Entrepreneur
VOICES
ON

THE SCIENCE
OF SUCCESS

The Staff of Entrepreneur Media, Inc.

Entrepreneur
PRESS

Entrepreneur Press, Publisher
Cover Design: Andrew Welyczko
Production and Composition: Eliot House Productions

This publication is designed to provide accurate and authoritative
information in regard to the subject matter covered. It is sold with the
understanding that the publisher is not engaged in rendering legal,
accounting or other professional services. If legal advice or other
expert assistance is required, the services of a competent professional
person should be sought.

Library of Congress Cataloging-in-Publication Data
    Names: Small, Jonathan J., editor. | Entrepreneur Media, Inc.
    Title: Entrepreneur voices on the science of success / by the staff of
        Entrepreneur Media, Inc.; edited by Jonathan Small.
    Description: Irvine, California: Entrepreneur Media, Inc., [2018]
    Identifiers: LCCN 2018022896 | ISBN 978-1-59918-634-4 (alk.
        paper) | ISBN 1-59918-634-9 (alk. paper)
    Subjects: LCSH: Success in business.
    Classification: LCC HF5386 .E56 2018 | DDC 658.4/09—dc23
    LC record available at https://lccn.loc.gov/2018022896

Printed in the United States of America
22 21 20 19   10 9 8 7 6 5 4 3 2 1

CONTENTS

Contents

Contents

PART III

STRATEGIES TO MOBILIZE AND MOTIVATE
   YOUR CUSTOMERS—REFLECTIONS

PART IV
MINDSETS THAT CREATE BALANCE

CHAPTER 29

STRESSED OUT? SCIENCE SAYS TO PLAY A
   VIDEO GAME FOR FIVE MINUTES
   by Stephen J. Bronner, news director at Entrepreneur

CHAPTER 30

NINE RESEARCH-BACKED WAYS TO TURN
   AROUND A BAD DAY
   by John Rampton, entrepreneur, connector, and online influencer

CHAPTER 31

SCIENCE SHOWS HOW CREATIVITY CAN
   REDUCE STRESS
   by Deepak Chopra and Kabir Sehgal, authors of
   Home: Where Everyone Is Welcome

CHAPTER 32

TO THRIVE IN WORK AND LIFE, HERE'S
   WHAT SCIENCE SAYS YOU NEED
   by Nina Zipkin, Entrepreneur Staff writer

FOREWORD BY BEN ANGEL

Marketing Expert and Bestselling Author

*W*hat do peak performers do that I don't? If the strategies of the ultra-successful are so great, then why do I fall short when I apply them?

If you've ever asked yourself these questions, know that you're not alone. I myself have learned over the years that the science of success isn't as black and white as the self-help gurus have led us to believe. They tell us to "quit making excuses" but fail to break down *why* we make excuses based on a deep understanding of not just psychology, but the science of success as a whole.

For years, I beat myself up wondering why I couldn't reach my goals sooner, if at all. It's only recently that I've been able to look beneath the surface and gain new insight as to why we do what we do and why some strategies work for some and fail miserably for others.

To find the answers to these questions, I traveled from Australia to the U.S. and Canada to interview top neuroscientists, biohackers, functional doctors, and psychologists to gain a comprehensive and complete understanding of the essence of the science of success. What I learned shocked me. Success cannot be distilled down into any one simple strategy like waking up at 5 A.M. each day or making your bed every morning. Instead, it's made up of a combination of strategies that only when applied in unison provide the catalyst for real breakthroughs to occur across every area of our businesses and lives.

You have likely compared yourself to your heroes to only ever feel like you come up short, you're not as productive as you'd like to be, you're easily overwhelmed, or you lack the structure to pull off your most ambitious goals. We've all been there. But you can get past questioning yourself and get to a place where you feel that success is not only possible, but probable. The bottom line is this: To unlock your capacity, you have to try many different keys until you find the ones that click for you. What works for a billionaire, you, or me is as individual as a fingerprint and must be treated as such.

But where do you start? Step one is in your hands.

Entrepreneur Voices on the Science of Success is a must-read book for anyone looking to re-energize themselves, increase their productivity, boost their confidence and rapidly transform their business. It presents science-backed research that you can easily experiment with and habits you can add to your routine—all without wasting hours reading about it online.

The strategies shared here are from the best of the best including experts like Deepak Chopra, CEOs of billion-dollar companies, business advisors, researchers, and the incredible *Entrepreneur* editorial team members who have dedicated their lives to helping millions fulfill their ambitions.

Know that you're in safe hands as you walk through actionable, bite-sized insights that will show you how to use neuroscience, brain hacks, and habits to help rewire your mind for success and change the way you tackle your entrepreneurial to-do list forever. You'll discover how to crush your goals, create powerful habits, become more likable, generate word-of-mouth marketing for your business, and build a billion-dollar company.

So, if you have an insatiable thirst to uncover how to turn yourself into a peak performer, this book will become a mainstay on your desk, especially when you need an injection of inspiration, an easy-to-apply strategy for dialing in your focus, or a path to rapidly growing your business.

If you're ready to see success in your business and life, grab a cup of coffee, pen, and paper, because your life is about to be transformed in ways you've never imagined.

ACHIEVE YOUR GOALS WITH SCIENCE

Is success a science? Like hitting a baseball or solving a math equation, can it be narrowed down into actionable nuggets of proven knowledge and skills that you can apply to your life and your business? These are the questions everyone—from scientists to academics, psychologists to sociologists—is studying at this very moment. And the answer, at least so far, is this: While science may not provide all the solutions, it is an essential ingredient in any business endeavor. To ignore or discount it is, well, scientifically shortsighted.

There is simply too much data and cutting-edge research available at your fingertips to not take advantage of it immediately. Through science, entrepreneurs are discovering new ways to increase their businesses' productivity, identify customer needs, and implement policies proven to attract and retain business. By studying how people engage with their products, they are creating customer-friendly tools and policies that are winning a new business and maximizing profits. By studying how high-performing individuals think and act, they are adopting principles and practices that lead to more fruitful and satisfying lives.

The science of success can be split into two categories: knowledge that can be applied to your life, and knowledge that can be applied to your business. The two are not mutually exclusive. In fact, a combination platter of the two can be the best course of action. So what are some things entrepreneurs can learn from science? While it's true that some entrepreneurs inherently possess certain essential traits such as confidence, passion, and dedication, we now know through neuroscience how to condition and rewire our brains to think in similar ways. Researchers also have a much better understanding of how we establish routines and habits. By pinpointing the biological reasons behind why we behave the way we do, they can recommend specific brain "hacks" to help us achieve our dreams. Thanks to science, we also have a better understanding of the importance of impressions and influence. New studies reveal fascinating insights on how to be more memorable—both in a good and a not-so-good way.

As much as science can help us understand ourselves, it is equally useful in helping entrepreneurs understand their businesses and their customers. Human psychology teaches us a great deal about how to interact with customers, both on and offline. And sophisticated data gives us more business intelligence than we believed possible even 10 years ago. Gone are the days of relying solely on your "gut instincts" to make decisions. Entrepreneurs are now loaded with as many facts and data points as they need to make informed choices.

This book lays out some of the cutting-edge and common-sense science available to you as a business owner. It is not a how-to guide to success. Think of it more as a buffet of fact-driven research that you can choose to ingest or ignore. Science cannot make you successful—only you can do that. But it can provide you with real and tangible data about the tactics, skills, knowledge, and routines of successful people in business. As one of the pre-eminent scientists of our time, Neil deGrasse Tyson, once said, "The good thing about science is that it's true whether or not you believe in it."

HABITS THAT INCREASE PRODUCTIVITY

Warren Buffett starts every morning poring over 500 pages of magazines, newspapers, and books. The first thing Tim Ferriss does when he wakes up is make his bed. Sheryl Sandberg makes sure to get to work at Facebook every day at 7 A.M. sharp. Like many highly successful entrepreneurs, all these business leaders have developed habits that they believe increase their focus and productivity.

And these are not just the eccentric quirks of multimillionaires. Increasingly, scientific studies show that by dropping bad habits and developing and bolstering good ones, you can set yourself up to achieve your goals and dreams.

Let's face it: The word "habit" gets a bad rap. From the time we're children, we're told to break habits, not build them. And as we become adults, most of us associate habits with negative routines, like constantly checking our smartphones, biting our nails, or drinking too much coffee. Those are not the habits we're talking about (although some studies have found that coffee is actually good for you). The habits of successful entrepreneurs broaden your mind, increase your energy and enthusiasm, and actually rewire your brain to think in a whole new way.

So which habits should you develop and which should you drop? Like breakfast cereal, habits come in all sorts of varieties and options. There are the habits we think are beneficial but are actually impeding our progress. Multitasking is a prime example. While most of us brag about our ability to juggle answering email, talking on the phone, and conducting a meeting at the same time, scientists are not impressed. In fact, studies show that interweaving two or more tasks is the least effective way to gain comprehension.

Then there are the habits that we think are detrimental, but are actually helpful. It is commonly believed that being a workaholic is a recipe for stress and anti-social behavior. And that's largely true for workaholics who hate their jobs. But studies have shown that people who put in long hours on the job, but who are engaged and enthusiastic about their work, tend to be happier and more productive than the stereotypical workaholic, who can suffer from health problems, sleep disorders, and depression.

Lastly, there are the habits that we might not have thought of, but that have been adopted by some of the most successful and fulfilled people in business. These are the behavioral modifications that, when practiced on a daily basis, can transform our performance from good to great.

From brain hacks to breaking bad habits, from small behavioral changes, like meditating 10 minutes every day, to larger commitments, such as spending 80 percent of your day reading like Warren Buffett, the following chapters lay out a science-backed road map to success.

1

NINE SCIENCE-BACKED INSIGHTS ON FINDING SUCCESS IN BUSINESS AND LIFE

Entrepreneur Staff

Whether at work or at home, success is something we strive for in all aspects of our lives. And while there are a number of obvious things you should be doing to achieve your goals, there are also some not-so-obvious ones. For example, we're often told that working too much can be detrimental to our health and wellness; however, a study found that high engagement actually protects from health risks associated with working too much. And being too happy around co-workers might make you seem naive, rather than simply optimistic.

From office jokes to sales leads to patience, check out these nine science-backed insights to help you achieve success.

1. Workaholism Has an Upside

Those who work more than 11 hours a day have been shown to have a higher risk of heart disease, high blood pressure, obesity, and high cholesterol. But there's better news for happy workaholics: High engagement may protect you from these risks. According to the *Harvard Business Review*, companies see a spike in productivity and a dip in turnover when workaholics are focused and content in their jobs.

2. Office Jokes Are Risky

According to a study by the Wharton School, humor can increase your status at work, make you appear more competent, and make you more likely to be elected as a group leader. But that's only if your jokes are appropriate. An off-color or bad joke can backfire and diminish your status, leaving co-workers thinking you're incompetent.

3. Dial Down the Happy

Employees who are too outwardly upbeat are seen as naive and unsophisticated. Why? Research finds that overly happy employees are perceived as more vulnerable to deception or exploitation. While it's good to be positive, it is not always motivating, inspiring, or even attractive to your co-workers. Instead, try to focus on being thoughtful and wise about the people and the world around you.

4. Experiment with Different Sales Techniques

When it comes to generating sales, you should be open to all sorts of different approaches. One size does not fit all. For example, to generate leads for its online course-building services, PLR.me tried using a chatbot—and found that 78 percent of people who engaged with it stayed through to the end.

5. Be Patient

In his TED Talk "What I Learned from 2,000 Obituaries," Lux Narayan, CEO of Unmetric, says, "We looked at the data: 2,000 editorial, nonpaid obituaries over a 20-month period between 2015 and 2016. What did these 2,000 deaths—rather, lives— teach us? The average age at which they achieved things is 37. What that means is, you've got to wait 37 years before your first significant achievement that you're remembered for, on average, 44 years later, when you die at the age of 81. Talk about having to be patient."

6. Go for Face Time

Despite the ease of digital communication, sometimes good, old-fashioned face time is the most effective communication technique. A study found face-to-face requests are 34 times more successful than emails.

7. Get Psyched Up

In his book *Psyched Up: How the Science of Mental Preparation Can Help You Succeed*, Daniel McGinn writes, "For people who suffer from extreme nerves . . . don't obsess over calming down. Instead, tell yourself that the sweaty palms and the racing heart are a positive sign, because they signify excitement: You're lucky to be here and to have this opportunity to prove how good you are."

8. More Is Better

"On average, creative geniuses [aren't] qualitatively better in their fields than their peers. They simply produced a greater volume of work, which gave them more variation and a higher chance of originality," writes Adam Grant in his book *Originals: How Non-Conformists Move the World.* "To generate a handful of masterworks, Mozart composed more than 600 pieces before his death at 35, Beethoven produced 650 in his lifetime . . . Einstein wrote papers on general and special relativity that transformed physics, but many of his 248 publications had minimal impact."

9. Get to Work

According to David Autor, professor of economics at MIT, "Many of the great inventions of the last 200 years were designed to replace human labor. Assembly lines were engineered to replace inconsistent human handiwork with machine perfection. Computers were programmed to swap out error-prone, inconsistent human calculation with digital perfection . . . And yet, the fraction of U.S. adults employed in the labor market is higher now in 2016 than it was 125 years ago." Machines may be able to do many of our jobs, but they haven't replaced us completely. So get started!

SCIENCE-BACKED BRAIN HACKS TO CRUSH YOUR GOALS

Kate Rockwood

Often, the hardest part of achieving success is when you transition your goals into habits. Goals tell you where you want to go, but habits give you the discipline you need to get there. It may seem daunting, but the process will get easier with time. All it takes now is persistence, passion, and a little science-backed knowledge to get you over the hump.

Here are seven tips that will help you keep pushing.

1. Get Bold

Want to push your performance to the max? Make a stretch goal, rather than one that's easily attainable. Stretch goals push you beyond your usual limits. Penn State psychology professors found in a study that big, lofty goals are correlated more strongly with improved performance than small, incremental goals. The higher the bar, the harder we push.

2. Narrow Your Focus

So you want to pitch 20 new clients, build out the product line, and scout a second location? Time to pare down that to-do list. In a study in the *Journal of Marketing Research*, participants who picked just one goal achieved success at nearly double the rate of those who chased two or three at a time.

3. Grab a Pen

Got a goal? Write it down. In a study at Dominican University, people who wrote down their objectives achieved roughly 50 percent more than people who merely thought about them.

4. Think in Ranges

A study published in the *Journal of Consumer Research* shows that setting a goal within a range (say, raising revenue 8 to 10 percent) makes you more likely to stick with it than if you aim for a flat number. Even better: "You'll be more likely to try to set a goal again in the future," says lead researcher Maura Scott, a professor at Florida State University.

5. Map It Out

A goal is great; a game plan is even better. In a study in the *Journal of Applied Psychology*, participants who spent two hours mapping out how they planned to achieve specific goals were more likely to find success. The researchers wrote: "Goal clarity increases persistence, making individuals less susceptible to the undermining effects of anxiety, disappointment, and frustration."

6. Enlist a Friend

An accountability buddy can work just as well in the boardroom as at the gym. Research shows that when people share weekly progress reports with a friend, their likelihood of success at reaching a goal climbs to 76 percent.

7. Cue the Immediate Gratification

Our brains naturally want to put off daunting tasks and let our future selves deal with them (the psych term for this is "present bias"). But a 2016 study in the *Chicago Booth Review* offers a way around your inner procrastinator: Give yourself small rewards in the near future to spur greater achievement of long-term goals. A slice of cake every time you cold-call an investor? A Friday-night Netflix binge every week you advance the ball on your big goal? Whatever keeps you inching toward the finish line!

8. Get Unmotivated

OK, it sounds completely counterintuitive, but a study by the *British Journal of Health Psychology* found that trying to motivate yourself to reach a goal was less effective than setting an intention for when and what you want to accomplish. Researchers reported that people who read motivational materials were less likely to get things done, while people who made a plan and followed through were much more successful.

By implementing these strategies into your regimen, you slowly train your brain to think about your goals and success in new ways. What may start off as a marathon eventually becomes a sprint.

WHY YOU SHOULD STOP SAYING SORRY, ACCORDING TO SCIENCE

Rose Leadem

If you hurt someone's feelings or turn someone down, saying sorry might not be the best solution. In fact, an apology might just add fuel to the fire, a study by researchers from Dartmouth College and the University of Texas has found.

To assess the impact of apologies after social rejections, researchers approached more than a thousand people, asked them questions, and had them participate in several experiments. When asked to write "a good way of saying no" to a social request, 39 percent of participants included an apology, with the belief that it would lighten the situation. However, when they were put on the receiving end of these notes, they reported feeling more hurt.

Apologies can actually anger people and trigger them to strike back, the researchers found. In another experiment, they conducted face-to-face rejections to understand how rejectees actually felt after an incident.

"People often don't want to admit that they have hurt feelings, so in some of the studies, we looked at how much people wanted to seek revenge," explains the study's lead author, Dr. Gili Freedman.

In the experiment, when rejected with an apology from participating in a taste test, rejectees got even: Many gave more hot sauce to the person who rejected them, after they were told the individual did not like spicy food.

It doesn't stop there. Whether sincere or not, when people receive apologies, they often feel like they have to forgive the person, even if they are not ready. After asking participants to watch videos of people being rejected, when a person received an apology along with the rejection, most viewers felt that person was obliged to forgive even if they didn't actually feel it.

"Our research finds that despite their good intentions, people are going about it the wrong way," Freedman says.

Even if you choose to apologize, you should realize that there is a science to saying, "I'm sorry." One study analyzed 183 public apologies from famous people. They found that when the apology included a denial (it wasn't me) or evasion (let's change the subject), it didn't sit well with fans, according to opinion polls. But when the apology contained elements of remorse (I'm mortified) or correction (I will never do this again) that was a more effective approach.

NINE PROVEN HABITS OF HIGHLY INNOVATIVE PEOPLE

Deep Patel

The biggest success stories always hinge on innovation and creating breakthroughs no one else achieved. The people behind these departures from the norm are revolutionaries; they are courageous enough to step away from the tried-and-true methods to carve their own way forward.

Innovative people disrupt whole industries with their ideas. Their brainchildren take on lives of their own and may impact generations to come. So what gives these super-creative people their edge? How do they tap into that talent? For one, they've learned to cultivate certain habits that support and heighten their creativity.

Here are nine proven habits that highly innovative people use daily.

1. Pursue Your Passions

Creative people tend to be intrinsically motivated, meaning that their drive comes from within. This internal desire spurs them to pursue their dreams.

Innovative people feel compelled to follow their passions. They are energized by challenging activities. Highly innovative and successful people aren't necessarily the most talented of the bunch, but they consistently and persistently go after their goals.

Others slack off because their motivation is extrinsic, or externally motivated by rewards such as money, fame, grades or praise. Internally driven motivation is usually most effective because the person desires to put in the work to succeed. This is strongly linked to the "Intrinsic Motivation Principle of Creativity," or the propensity for creativity to flourish when people are motivated by personal enjoyment of the work itself.

2. Keep a Book of Ideas

The most successful and creative people are often obsessive note takers. They have a habit of writing things down, whether it's a stroke of genius that came to them in a moment of inspiration or an interesting concept they read about. As great as your memory might be, when an insight comes to you, it's always best to put it into written form so you can go back and evaluate it later.

Creative people also tend to be doodlers and list makers. They jot down to-do lists, places they want to visit and books they want to read so they can refer to them later.

3. The More Hours You Work, the More Productive You Are

Just because you're working for 8, 10, or even 12 hours a day doesn't mean you're productive. Between breaks, distractions and fatigue, the average employee working an eight-hour workday is only really productive for portions of the day.

Furthermore, working too many hours can be detrimental to your health. According to a study of 85,000 people in the European Heart Journal, long working days can increase the odds of you having a stroke. Working more hours does not automatically mean you will get more done. Instead, block out times when you can work undisrupted by turning off notifications or closing your office door.

Furthermore, make sure that you schedule time for breaks. Taking a breather will help you recharge and refocus so that you can get back to the task at hand. More on that in a bit.

4. You Work Best Under Pressure

Some people claim that working under pressure boosts their productivity. That may be true in small doses. For example, you may have an upcoming trip and you need to hustle so you can get away. Living like this on a consistent basis however isn't sustainable and usually only creates stress.

Stress impairs both your health and work. It's long been linked to cardiovascular problems, and can certainly make you less fun to work with. Because of all this, keep stress to a minimum. One healthy tip is to not wait until the last minute. Be aware of deadlines and set priorities to help with this.

5. Jumping Right in Will Help You Get More Done

Some people recommend that you just jump right into your work, without a plan. The idea is that as long as you're getting work done, you're making progress.

This can be both true and not true. You may end-up working on a key project for an entire day without having accomplished, or even started, any of your other key tasks. You were so focused on getting certain items done that you did it all without a plan. That's like driving across the country without a map or using GPS.

A more productive approach would be to kick off your day by identifying key tasks and mapping out work time. That takes some preparation, but it will help you stay on track when you come across obstacles.

6. You Must Keep Working Until You're Done with a Task

I get it. Why start a project if you aren't going to finish it?

Because, sometimes stopping isn't a bad thing. Instead of forcing yourself to finish a task—even if you've hit a wall—identify a good place to stop and switch gears to another item on your to-do-list. For example, if you've been doing data analysis all morning, take a break and respond to some important emails. This allows your brain to take a break from a problem it's been tackling. When you return to the original task you may be refreshed enough to crank it out more quickly and effectively.

7. Multitasking Is Efficient

I can understand the theory. Working on two or three projects at the same time means you're getting more done. Unfortunately, multitasking just isn't possible.

"The neuroscience is clear: We are wired to be mono-taskers," writes Cynthia Kubu, PhD, and Andre Machado, MD. "One study found that just 2.5 percent of people are able to multitask effectively. And when the rest of us attempt to do two complex activities simultaneously, it is simply an illusion."

If you take a good look at the times you've multi-tasked, you probably see that you switched focus from one thing to another too often to do either of them very well. This is deadly from a productivity standpoint.

In short, don't multitask. Do one task at a time and then move-on to the next.

8. Rewards Boost Productivity

While monetary or physical rewards can be used to boost productivity, they usually only last momentarily. Once a reward has been received, we eventually return to the same level of productivity.

Instead of relying solely on rewards and incentives, tap into your intrinsic motivation. What about a task is important to you and requires your effort? This probably motivates us more than any type of physical reward can.

To get started, get in touch with your life's purpose. This is key when it comes to self-motivation. If you're not passionate or excited about whatever you're doing, then why bother at all? You may find that the more fulfilled you feel by the work you're doing, the more productive you are.

9. Productivity Techniques Will Solve All of Your Problems

Go back and review any article providing productivity advice. You're bound to see techniques like the Pomodoro Technique or Jerry Seinfeld's "Don't Break the Chain."

Don't get me wrong. These techniques can be effective. That's why people swear by them. However, just because it works for them doesn't mean it's going to work for you. So, don't force yourself to use a productivity technique that isn't working for you.

Try out a different technique until you find the ones that work best for you. Personally, I live-by the Pomodoro Technique, which is working for around

25 minutes and then taking a five minute break (or a bit longer).

This can be altered to suit your specific work habits. For example, I can often work straight for an hour before I start losing focus. So, I sometimes work for 60-minutes straight and then take a 30-minute break.

As you can see, it's all about what works for you. Keep this in mind as you test these productivity myths, and find the truth in them that helps you get more done.

SEVEN SCIENCE THINGS YOU MUST DO TO BUILD A BILLION-DOLLAR COMPANY

Chirag Kulkarni

When I started Taco, I knew I wanted to grow it into a billion-dollar company. But realistically, I knew that creating a billion-dollar company meant I had to impact billions of people and not just focus on metrics, like the bottom line.

To build a billion-dollar company, a founder must have a billion-dollar mindset and practice certain daily habits that science has found to be the common denominators among the world's wealthiest businesspeople. Scientific research has confirmed specific actions are more likely to assist you in generating wealth.

Check out these seven actions you will want to work on—and achieve daily—if you want to hit the billion-dollar mark.

1. Read

Today's billionaires have a voracious appetite for reading. They consume many pages and books in a short amount of time. Warren Buffett actually spends the majority of every day reading books, articles, and online content to better understand the business environment and the factors that impact investing and strategic decisions.

Reading provides critical knowledge that can help businesspeople move their company to the next level of revenue. It also opens their eyes to possibilities and patterns that can benefit their organization in terms of new directions and revenue streams.

2. Obsess

Successful people are passionate, but those who want to take their companies to the next level are actually obsessed with what they are doing.

Passion involves telling others about what you are creating, but you know you are obsessed when other people start pointing out your behavior. If you are up all night working on the company's strategy, then you are obsessed. You'll also have a better chance of keeping on top of all the details and really propelling your business, your money, and yourself forward.

But be aware—idea overload can severely damage your business. This is when you have so many ideas that you fail to organize and prioritize them, causing you to be confused, overwhelmed, and, well, overloaded. Obsess, but focus.

3. Meet

Take the time to meet someone new every day. This person doesn't necessarily have to be in your industry or even in business at all. It's more about identifying people in our daily lives that are least like ourselves, in a completely different field, or not even interested in business. One of my friends, Sujan Patel, did this, and it helped him generate $198,000 in revenue for his marketing company.

This is the best way to understand other perspectives and learn something new in order to grow your business, attract talent that can fill in those gaps, and gain a better, fine-tuned understanding of your audience. Getting to know others who work outside your expertise and who do things differently can help you look at things in an unexpected way.

4. Be Humble

Nice guys don't finish last. In fact, those who focus on their humility are the ones who slip under the radar and come out on top. This is because they are looking to help others, not spend time broadcasting what they are doing.

You don't need to prove anything to others. That's why you are putting all your energy into making the company more successful. Billionaires realize that they are not doing all this work for themselves but to do something that changes the world or makes it a better place. And they don't need to seek approval and admiration for doing so.

Many people were initially surprised to find out that Mark Zuckerberg was a billionaire. That's because he doesn't talk about it. Every day, remind yourself how fortunate you are to be where you are, and remember who helped you and your business get there.

5. Question

You can only reach that high-level status with your company if you are never satisfied with the current results. When you question everything and seek out answers that push the envelope, you are a step closer to hitting the billion-dollar range. When a company settles for their current results, they are essentially not interested in raising the bar on revenues. However, when a leader questions those results and wonders if more could be done, the door opens, and they can start moving from millionaire to billionaire.

6. Connect

A billionaire understands the need to connect the dots of their business with the assistance from mentors, partners, and others who have leads or stakeholders who might provide some benefit.

While most people understand the value of networking, billionaires have maxed out on the connector moves to ensure that they have made every possible connection for pushing the needle forward on the business. They have made it their complete focus to see how others can help the business in ways not previously explored to raise their revenues and create that billion-dollar company. Find a way to make a new connection through professional networks, either in life or online, every day.

7. Start

Get going before everyone else and work daily to stay ahead of the crowd. Sir Richard Branson just decided to go ahead and start a company even if there were questions about money or whether it was possible to succeed. He just rolled up his sleeves and dug in, believing it would work itself out. More important was the need to get started before anyone else and beat them to market.

That magic moment where you know you are really ready will never come, so it's more important to take the leap and go—just move!—once you have some idea of what you are doing. Billionaires get there first, not last or even second. Start something new every day, whether it is a hobby, a different exercise routine, or a new business initiative.

While all levels of businesses and leaders may practice these habits to a certain extent, only those who do them every day and to the fullest have been able to move up to billion-dollar status. Taking advantage of them and making the right moves every day will also turn them into healthy habits that serve your business—and yourself—well.

6

NEUROSCIENCE TELLS US HOW TO HACK OUR BRAINS FOR SUCCESS

John Rampton

What's the secret to success? Some would argue that insanely successful people possess common traits like having a vision, showing gratitude, being honest, learning from failure, and having a high emotional intelligence.

While these traits definitely play a role, the real secret to success comes down to science, particularly advances in neuroscience, and how you can condition your brain to achieve your goals and dreams.

The neuroscience of success can get complicated, but it comes down to how your brain functions in three different areas: the reticular activating system (RAS), the release of dopamine, and your memory. If you're not a science person, I'll try to make this all as painless as possible.

The Reticular Activating System

Located at the base of the brain where it connects with the spinal cord is one of the most important parts of the brain: the reticular activating system.

The RAS influences cognition and basically acts as a filter for the roughly 8 million bits of information subconsciously flowing through our brain. In other words, it eliminates the white noise. When a message gets past the RAS filter, it enters the cerebrum and is converted into conscious thoughts, emotions, or both.

As Ruben Gonzalez, author of *The Courage to Succeed*, explains, "Even though the cerebrum is the center of thought, it will not respond to a message unless the RAS allows it. The RAS is like Google. There are millions of websites out there, but you filter out the ones you are not interested in simply by typing a keyword."

So what messages get through? Pretty much just the ones that are currently important to you. For example, if you're focused on preparing for a speaking engagement, your RAS is going to filter in the thoughts that will make your presentation a success, such as the tools and resources you'll need to deliver a memorable speech.

Gonzalez adds, "This means the more you keep your goals 'top of mind,' the more your subconscious mind will work to reach them. That's why writing your goals down every day, visualizing your intended outcome, and regularly saying affirmations is so important! Doing those things truly does help you to focus your subconscious mind on what's important to you."

Dopamine Feedback Loops

While RAS can help you focus on the outcome you'd like to achieve, the release of dopamine is what makes success feel oh-so-good.

As Mark Lukens, founding partner of recruiting company Method3, wrote in an article, "When we succeed at something, our brains release chemical rewards, the most important of which is the neurotransmitter dopamine, a chemical best known for the role it plays in addiction and drug use." Dopamine, despite this negative association, "is a natural part of how our brains function, producing the sensation of pleasure whenever you taste coffee or chocolate, or when you achieve a big win."

Because of this, it makes sense that "dopamine is strongly connected to motivation, driving us to repeat the behaviors that create that rush, even when we aren't experiencing it." However, the dopamine response is short-term, but since our brains remember how awesome it was before, we seek it out again and again.

That's when dopamine loops enter the picture. After you've experienced repeated success, the pleasure you initially had gets smaller and smaller. Think of it this way: After you've already beaten a video game, it just doesn't feel as good the second or third time you win, right? That's when you seek out bigger rewards, like unlocking trophies, new characters, or swag when completing a level.

"Under the right circumstances, this can drive us to seek out ever-greater thrills," adds Lukens. It's why video game players are constantly engaged, it's the reason you check your phone every minute for likes after updating your Facebook status, and it's what motivates us to accomplish bigger and better things.

For instance, if your goal was to acquire three new clients within two weeks, your next goal would be to acquire six new clients in one week. As an added perk, this also helps you weed out the work and goals that aren't motivating you or your team.

Memories

Neuroscientists who have studied the way the brain retrieves memories say this can also determine success.

Think about that time you went mountain biking and had a nasty spill. That was a bad experience that might discourage you from mountain biking again, at least for the foreseeable future. The same is true with starting a business. If it failed, you will be more hesitant about taking that risk again.

Scientists, however, have found that we can edit those bad memories to remove the negative associations. In fact, this memory therapy is used to treat PTSD sufferers. You can also edit good memories to further propel you toward success.

To weaken bad memories, bring that memory back to your mind and then let it get smaller and dimmer, like you're watching an old black-and-white TV fade out. Once there, insert new details that scramble the memory. For instance, think about the time you bombed while giving a speech or investor pitch. Now imagine that your audience was dressed in scuba gear. Do that five or ten times, and that memory will make you chuckle instead of wince.

As for strengthening your memories, recall the good memories as bright and loud as possible, like watching a movie in an IMAX theater. Keep adding to how great that experience made you feel for five or ten repetitions. You should now feel on top of the world, and can use it to motivate yourself going forward.

Hacks to Rewire Your Brain for Success

The good news is that you can actually rewire your brain to become more successful. In fact, according to neuroscientist Michael Merzenich, it takes just 30 hours of training, using specific neuroscience techniques, to improve your memory, cognition, speech patterns, and reading comprehension.

I know that may sound like a lot. But it's just an hour a day for a month to achieve lifelong success. That's totally worth it. And most of this training involves simple daily tasks.

Eight Simple Steps to Success

1. *Exercise and meditation.* Exercising releases endorphins, which can help with problem solving and boost creativity. Meditation can help you achieve inner calm and break down any mental barriers or limitations.
2. *Consume a diet rich in omega-3s and healthy fats.* These can help keep dopamine levels in your brain active, as well as increase cerebral circulation.

3. *Precision affirmations.* "We've all heard of affirmations: repeating positive statements to ourselves in order to believe them," writes John Assaraf, CEO of NeuroGym. "While that may sound good in theory, there is often a severe lack of specificity that can hinder results." Instead, "make a clear, definitive statement about yourself as if it is already true; your subconscious mind takes over and will act in accordance with that belief." This "will imprint these beliefs into new neural pathways."

4. *Say your "chief aim" every morning and evening.* Based on Napoleon Hill's *Think and Grow Rich*, "A definite chief aim is a specific, clearly defined statement of purpose," writes educator and speaker Julie Connor. "It has the power to guide your subconscious mind. It transforms your attitude from pessimism into positive expectation." Write down your own "chief aim" and say it out loud every morning and evening. When I started my invoice company, I started every day by saying that I would become the best at this. I'm not quite there, but I'm getting there.

5. *Get plenty of sleep.* Make sure you get between six and eight hours of quality sleep every night so you're more attentive and focused.

6. *15 minutes a day.* Carve out 15 minutes of your day to learn something new or improve a skill you already have. It will have a positive impact on your brain.

7. *Remove yourself from negative and stressful environments.* According to Robert Sapolsky, a professor of neurology at Stanford University, "stress can not only be stopped, but reversed once the source, psychological or physical, is removed or sufficiently reduced." In other words, the physical environment around us plays a very important role in the health of our brains.

8. *Visualization.* "Visualization is a powerful tool to retrain your subconscious mind, because it allows you to feel and experience a situation which hasn't happened yet—as if it were real," writes Assaraf. In short, "if you are able to genuinely 'see' yourself as financially successful in your mind, your subconscious will process that as reality."

The brain is incredibly complex, and scientists are continuously trying to unravel its mysteries. But, thanks to new research, we understand much more today than we did even ten years ago. One can only imagine what we'll know about the brain ten years from now.

SEVEN SCIENCE-BACKED STRATEGIES FOR BUILDING POWERFUL HABITS

Lydia Belanger

Achieving a goal often involves developing a new routine and sticking to it. Whether you want to network more, take on more consulting work, wake up earlier, or start exercising regularly, you'll have to cement your intention by making it a habit.

Switching up your schedule can be unsettling and inconvenient. Life gets in the way, and it can be tempting to make excuses about why you have to break your habit.

That's why some scientists dedicate their careers to figuring out what influences human behavior. If we understand how we're hard-wired to respond to our own actions, we can set ourselves up for continued success.

Read on for some scientifically proven tips for developing habits that last.

1. Discover What Triggers You

In his book *The Power of Habit*, author Charles Duhigg describes a simple neurological loop at the core of every habit, a revelation MIT researchers originally discovered. The three steps in the loop are "cue," "routine," and "reward."

To carry out a specific action regularly, you'll need a reliable reminder (the *cue*). If you aim to stick to a certain time of day, set an alarm. A consistent location also helps. Places you already frequent will likely trigger your existing habits (e.g., sitting on the couch makes you want to watch TV), so try to choose a new location to establish a new habit.

Other people are some of your biggest behavioral influences and can be cues, too. Try to surround yourself with individuals who already behave the way you aspire to.

If you perform on cue again and again, you'll develop your *routine*. And once you're immersed in your routine, you'll start to reap the *reward* that comes from following through on your intentions.

2. View Your Goal as an Obligation Rather Than a Desire

Sometimes we're motivated more by the negative repercussions of *not* doing something than by the possible benefits of doing it.

E. Tory Higgins, a professor of psychology and business at Columbia University, has spent more than 20 years studying what makes people reach their goals. He serves as the director of Columbia's Motivation Science Center, which has studied the principles behind motivating people since 2002. He describes two types of goals: promotional goals and prevention goals. Promotional goals are ones we hope to achieve, while prevention goals are ones we are afraid not to achieve.

You can look at the same goal and frame it in a promotional manner or a prevention manner. Higgins has said that prevention is more effective. So tell yourself, "I have to achieve my goal because otherwise I won't X." The first time you carry out the activity necessary for your habit and goal, it will become your new status quo, and you will feel worried that slipping up at any point in the future will disrupt that status quo.

Conversely, framing it in a promotional way, such as "I have to achieve my goal so that X good thing will happen," doesn't hold you accountable. If you have an off day, you may start to feel that the "X good thing" you're working toward will never materialize, and you'll be less likely to keep going.

3. Work on One Habit at a Time

Even if you've determined your triggers and a schedule for carrying out your new habit, you will be far less likely to keep it up if you try to make more than one big change in your routine at a time.

If you're trying to master more than one habit, studies have shown you'll be far more likely to fail than if you're just working on one. You don't need to revamp your entire life all at once.

4. Stack One Habit on Top of Another

Keep in mind that you already have a lot of habits, but don't worry: They don't have to get in the way of the new ones you're trying to establish.

In fact, your existing habits can serve as the basis for your future ones. Certain actions are already second nature to you—from showering to brewing a pot of coffee—because you have developed neural pathways in your brain that take you through the steps almost automatically.

Experts suggest that you "stack" your habits. For example, if your new goal is to practice gratitude regularly, when you go to the kitchen to make your coffee in the morning, you might think of one thing you're grateful for. Why try to carve a new path when you can follow a well-worn one?

5. Don't Confuse Your Habit with Your Goal

In other words, don't dwell on what you're working toward in the long run. If you successfully perform your habitual task, consider that a win in and of itself.

This is the "routine" part of the neurological habit loop. You can't expect to see dramatic fitness results after going to the gym a few times; the same goes for any other type of habit. Focus on the ritual, rather than the result. Over time, the process will become second nature, and your desired outcome will follow.

6. Minimize Decision Making

Making choices is tiresome. There's even a term for the exhaustion you feel after making too many: decision fatigue.

One study published in the *Journal of Personality and Social Psychology* found that participants demonstrated reduced self-control—less physical stamina, reduced persistence in the face of failure, and more procrastination—after making several decisions about what types of goods to buy.

If your goal is to read more, for instance, create a short list of books or articles you're interested in and then rank them in order of which you want to read first. Simply wandering over to your bookshelf every time you're ready to crack open a book will make you feel overwhelmed.

Streamlining your routine and narrowing your choices in as many aspects of your life as possible will save your mental energy for the activity you're trying to turn into a habit.

7. Reward Yourself

This doesn't mean you need to provide yourself with external rewards such as small personal gifts (although you might find that effective). Your brain chemistry has its own reward system.

Every time you check off a task on your to-do list, your brain secretes the hormone dopamine, which corresponds with pleasure, learning, and motivation. This is what makes you feel good about yourself when you do something you intended to do.

In pursuit of more dopamine, you'll be driven to perform that task again. Success begets success.

And keep in mind that little successes build up to big ones, as Stanford researcher B.J. Fogg has found. For instance, if your goal is better time management, commit to working on a project for just 10 minutes a day at first. If you set the bar at a height you can consistently clear, you'll be more likely to succeed, get that dopamine rush, and keep your momentum going.

FOUR SCIENCE-BACKED WAYS TO INCREASE PRODUCTIVITY

Murray Newlands

There is a ton of advice out there about how to strengthen your productivity, from eating more vegetables to making more lists. Everyone claims to have the answers. But knowing what will really work takes more than just reading; it takes scientific inquiry and proven studies.

I've put together this list of scientifically proven methods of boosting your productivity for those of you who want the facts, and just the facts. Use these methods in confidence, knowing you're giving your body and mind what they need to do your best work.

1. Work in Natural Light

According to a study done by the neuroscience program at Northwestern University, there is a strong relationship between workplace daylight exposure and office workers' sleep, activity, and quality of life.

The study found that employees who worked in natural light slept on average 46 more minutes per night, slept more soundly and efficiently, and reported higher quality of life scores than those who did not. Windowless workers had lower scores in measurements of physical problems and vitality than those who worked near daylight. They also had poorer outcomes in measures of overall sleep quality, sleep disturbances, and daytime dysfunction.

It's well-documented that a lack of natural light can disrupt the body's circadian rhythms, which can cause abnormal sleep patterns and seasonal affective disorder, leading to depression and lethargy, among other symptoms. All the ways lack of light affects the body can greatly reduce your productivity and energy.

If you don't work in an office with windows, you can buy a lamp that simulates natural light or find a new job where you can see the light.

2. Work for 90 Minutes at a Time

Working in shorter chunks of time instead of working for hours at a singular task has been proved to stimulate the brain, making you more productive in the long run.

Research has shown that our brains get very sleepy in the mornings, almost every 90 minutes. So you can work more efficiently when you break your time into a ratio of 90:20—90 minutes of work before taking a 20-minute break. This allows you to get into what's called a "flow state" when creativity is running at its optimum level, and then rest your brain when it's tired so you're fresh for the next 90 minutes.

3. Get Happy

Though most people think success will create happiness, it turns out that very much the opposite is true. A leading researcher in happiness, Sonja Lyubomirsky, studied the correlation between happiness and productivity in her book *The How of Happiness*.

She concluded that happiness has many positive outcomes that no one could predict—ones beyond joy, love, and contentment. When we're happy, we experience more energy, higher engagement with work, better relationships, higher self-esteem and stronger mental and physical health.

In sum, creating your own happiness translates to a better life, which in turn translates to higher productivity. The happier and healthier you are, the more you can do.

4. Take a Nap

You may think naps are only for the very young and the very aged, but science has proved that naps are incredibly good for productivity.

Science Says Naps Are the Answer

For one thing, naps keep you from burning out. David K. Randall writes in his book *Dreamland* that research subjects who napped showed greater emotional resilience and improved cognitive function. NASA research has shown that a short, 26-minute nap enhances performance by 34 percent and overall alertness by 54 percent.

Harvard sleep researcher Robert Stickgold says that napping also makes people more effective problem solvers. His research has shown that napping helps people "separate important information from extraneous details," especially when taken at midday to help get over afternoon fatigue.

Your productivity can change for the better; you have control over it. There are many tips and tricks available to you. But don't take my word for it. Try these scientifically backed ideas and see if they work for you.

HOW TO FIX OUR CONSTANT CONNECTIVITY, WHICH IS HURTING PRODUCTIVITY

Jennifer L. Gibbs and Terri R. Kurtzberg

Telling someone to "just put down the phone" these days is a lot like telling them to get more exercise or eat more vegetables. We all know that distraction and multitasking are eating away at our days, and we say we miss the simpler times when we had the chance to focus on people and ideas more singularly and thoroughly. And yet in the same breath, we defend the need to have our phones in hand to look at incoming messages—after all, there are important work matters to handle, family members with vital questions, and innumerable forms of entertainment to fill in the otherwise boring spaces in our lives. This is efficient! It's important! It's even satisfying to feel like we can keep all these plates spinning simultaneously.

Entrepreneurs in particular are prone to these behaviors. After all, a new business is like a new baby—it doesn't stop needing you just because you want a break, or because someone or something else is clamoring for your attention. However, our strongly held belief that we can (and do) handle all the interruptions and multitasking that we attempt all day long is false. What follows are three of the ways that our current patterns of activity are failing us, and what we can do about them.

1. Multitasking Is an Illusion

Our brains actually cannot process two different streams of thought at once. Instead, we rapidly pull the lever back and forth between two (or more) things, missing some of each and hoping to string together enough of what's left to make something coherent and functional at the end. Complicating the issue is the fact that our brains need a few moments to finish reviewing and processing any one conversation after it ends before they're ready to attend to something new, or even return to something else already in progress.

2. You're Not as Good as You Think You Are at Multitasking

Fascinating work has shown that those who spend the most time interweaving two or more tasks are actually the least effective cognitively at maintaining high-level comprehension of either task (despite tremendous confidence in their ability to do just that). Instead, they've just forgotten what it feels like to be able to focus on one thing, so they assume they're being successful when they aren't.

We all know multitasking can be addictive, but how it plays out is quite interesting. The brain, used to the constant "high" of receiving new stimulation, constantly seeks it out even when the individual is attempting to bring "laser focus" to a single task, and instead gets distracted by noticing every available sound, movement, or stray thought.

The notification alert of an incoming message can be as distracting as pausing to read the message itself. Indeed, even seeing your phone changes the way your brain works. To truly give yourself a chance to learn to refocus on one thing when needed, you must turn off noises and notifications and hide your devices behind a closed door or drawer. Start by rewarding yourself for going a small number of minutes without needing to check in or respond, and work up to larger blocks of time.

3. Americans Are "Accomplishment Junkies"

Nearly every minute of our waking lives, whether at work or at leisure, is filled with to-do lists and goal-oriented activities. We even foist this upon our children, whose school days are crammed with tests and whose extracurricular activities all now come complete with levels to pass, competitions to enter, and trophies to win. The standard American answer to the question "How are you?" has become "Busy!" as if running at maximum speed at all times is a badge of honor.

This is not the case everywhere. In other regions of the world, people accept maintaining relationships as an end in itself and can set aside tasks and goals in favor of just spending time with others. Needless to say, our stress rates far surpass those with this type of mindset. While you can't change your entire culture just by recognizing its foibles, it is useful to realize that the goal of using time efficiently can be a trap, and there are indeed other ways to live.

10

BREAKING THE BAD HABITS HOLDING YOU BACK WITH SCIENCE

Thai Nguyen

Bad habits can be like weeds in the garden: You get rid of them for a while, but they come right back. In order to successfully break a bad habit, you need to get to the roots.

A U.S. Army major stationed in Kufa during the Iraq War was given the task of curbing the violent riots in the local plazas. Instead of sending his troops in gung ho with gunfire, the major simply had the food vendors removed. And the riots ceased.

When the major was asked how he knew removing the food vendors would put an end to the riots, his answer was, "Understanding habits." Crowds would gather; after a few hours they would grow hungry, but with the food vendors gone, they would get discouraged and drift home. By removing one simple aspect, he broke the chain of events and eliminated the cycle that led to the riots.

You can break your bad habits with the same strategy. Charles Duhigg, author of *The Power of Habit*, explains the three key stages of habit formation:

The cue: This is the trigger that initiates the behavior, which becomes the habit. It could be a time of day when you drive past the doughnut shop or a social-media notification that leads you to procrastination. It is the spark that leads to the routine.

The routine: The routine is the actual behavior. Duhigg gives a personal example—at 3:30 p.m. each day, he'd look at the clock and get a craving for a cookie. He'd then go to the cafeteria, buy a cookie, and eat it while chatting with co-workers. That was his habitual routine.

The reward: The reward is the release of brain chemicals following your specific routine. This is what reinforces your "bad" behavior. Your brain is experiencing "happy chemicals" even though you're doing something you want to stop doing.

Now that we have deconstructed the habit, here are two steps to break it:

1. Deconstruct

Using the three stages of cue, routine, and reward, you need to deconstruct your bad habits. Uncover what your triggers are, take a step back, and look at the automated routine you're engaging in; then realize that you're giving yourself a false reward.

You need to pinpoint your moments of weakness. This means being honest with yourself. Keep in mind that removing just one of the three key factors can be enough to break down the entire bad habit.

For Duhigg, his real reason for getting the cookie wasn't that he craved sugar, but simply that he enjoyed chatting with his co-workers. When he realized he could socialize without buying a cookie, he broke the bad habit.

2. Replace or Redeem

Some habits need to be stopped cold turkey. Other habits can be replaced with healthier options or redeemed with slight alterations. Rather than snacking on Reese's Pieces, have some dark chocolate. If you chew on your nails when you are nervous, carry some chewing gum with you. Instead of checking your social media accounts, read an intellectually stimulating article online.

Start today. Now that you know the three key stages of habit formation, you can work on breaking down your bad habits immediately.

FIVE BAD HABITS YOU MUST CHANGE TO BE MORE PRODUCTIVE

Ahmed Safwan

Productivity is very important in today's fast-moving world. Most people try to add to their routine to get more done, but that approach takes a while before it yields good, measurable results.

Most of the time, all you need to triple your productivity is to stop doing a few things. Almost immediately, you'll see and feel a huge difference. Cutting out tasks that drag you down leaves space for the things that really matter. It might seem counterintuitive, but it makes sense to pare down first—and then begin integrating new systems into your life.

If you're looking for a place to start, consider how you're spending your time and concentrate on eliminating these five bad habits first. Use this free cheat sheet to help keep you accountable.

1. Scheduling Every Second of Your Day (with No Free Time)

This may come as a surprise, but if you want to start improving your productivity, you need to stop scheduling every second of your day. People enjoy the process of setting their calendar and the fleeting feeling of accomplishment it brings. But if you schedule too much, you'll end up hating your workdays.

In addition, when an emergency pops up or you don't have the energy to finish the remaining work, you'll lose track of your day. Your schedule will be a mess, and you won't achieve nearly as much as you'd set out to complete.

The solution? Opt for a simpler method, such as picking six important tasks you want to finish before you go to sleep. When you wake up, create a simple outline for the things you want to accomplish, but don't stick too rigidly to the schedule.

Listen to what your body is telling you. Keep your sights on the most important tasks—and don't forget to eat breakfast in the morning.

2. Trying to Succeed at Multiple Things at Once

This is where most people tend to lose focus. We all want to be successful in many aspects of life: build businesses for multiple markets, be an athlete, travel the world, and so on.

But if you follow too many opportunities at the same time, you're setting yourself up to fall short in more ways than one. Or, if you do achieve success, the law of distribution means you'll have little celebrations that don't bring as much satisfaction as one or two big wins.

It's better to identify one thing that will help you achieve other goals and focus all your energy on that catalyst for change. When you succeed, reduce the time you devote to that pursuit and redirect those hours or even minutes to other avenues.

The best part? You can leverage your initial success to help you reach other milestones. For example, if you build that business you've been thinking about starting and turn a consistent profit, you can use that success and capital to fuel other endeavors—making them successful twice as quickly as your first company. Or use your net proceeds to travel the world without worrying about cash flow or needing to spend time taking care of your business.

3. Aiming for Perfection

You know the feeling that nags you when you try to launch a new project? The twinge when you go live with a new website and then find a few small details that aren't quite perfect?

If you're like me, you're willing to spend hours or even days chasing the idea of perfection. But I've noticed a comical snowball effect that happens every time: When I start fixing one thing, I find a bunch of other things that need to be perfect, too. The loop keeps going long after I've run out of energy to do my best work. And that can lead to indefinite delays.

The bittersweet truth is no one will notice your imperfections the way you do. Even if a few people do pick up on a detail here and there, your losses won't be as severe as they will if you don't try at all. Even if you fail, you'll learn something.

Instead, aim to get your project to 90 percent— and then launch. You can iterate and make tweaks as you go.

4. Skipping Breaks to Get More Done

When you work more, you get more done, right? (Trick question. It's 100 percent wrong.)

As Cal Newport demonstrates in his book *Deep Work: Rules for Focused Success in a Distracted World*, the things you get done are equal to the time spent, minus the intensity of the work.

So if you spend ten hours doing things at an intensity of two, you'll achieve the same result as if you spend two hours doing things at an intensity of ten. It's an amazing concept. In one-fifth of the time, you achieved the same thing. The key to accomplishing more is increasing your intensity.

To get in the habit, you can follow the Pomodoro Technique. Work uninterruptedly on a single task for 25 minutes and then take a five-minute break. After four cycles, you can take a longer break, say 20 to 30 minutes. This is one of the three steps that helped me build my business while studying dentistry.

5. Not Rewarding Yourself

How does rewarding yourself increase productivity? It inspires you to sustain that level of intensity. And if you want to get more done, you need to build in more rewards.

When you've accomplished two hours of high-intensity work, reward yourself with something simple—like chocolate. You can even schedule free time in your calendar to enjoy these rewards. A longer burst of intense work might earn you a new movie, for example.

Trust me when I say it's very important to take time for these moments. If you don't, you'll burn out quickly. Scheduling rewards in advance not only prevents you from reaching that critical point but also helps you focus intently on the task at hand. You know you've allotted yourself time to do the work, and you also know you'll soon be enjoying a hard-won reward. Savor it.

ENTREPRENEUR VOICES SPOTLIGHT: INTERVIEW WITH BEN ANGEL

Marketing Expert and Bestselling Author

Australian marketing guru Ben Angel is the bestselling author of CLICK, *Sleeping Your Way to The Top in Business, Flee 9 to 5, and Unstoppable: A 90-Day Plan to Biohack Your Mind and Body for Success.* Founder of benangel.co, he offers entrepreneurs online marketing courses and expert guidance on such topics as building your personal brand, attracting new customers, and generating a sizable social media following.

Ben's career trajectory is a study in perseverance and experimentation. After dropping out of school at the age of 17, he embarked on a series of odd jobs, including running a metal sculpture business, organizing speed dating events targeting the gay market, and working in a mattress store. He struggled in his younger years with anxiety and confusion over his sexuality, but he eventually found his true calling as an inspirational speaker and writer. Always fascinated by the latest science and research, Ben talks to us about what he's learned over the years.

Entrepreneur: What are some of the habits you've developed that have led you to success?

Angel: Growing up on a cattle and cropping farm in South Australia, I learned from a very young age that consistency was king. This included reading and researching new business and personal-development strategies weekly and investing every last dollar I had in personal development, working out in the gym daily, and eating healthily six days a week. As simple as this foundation is, it has helped me get through some of my most traumatic life experiences, including the loss of my father to brain cancer. I know that no matter what happens in my life, if I look after myself and my health, everything will eventually fall into place. Knowing and trusting that everything is going to work out as it's meant to cannot be overstated. I have used these hypnosis and daily visualization practices my adult life.

Entrepreneur: Do you have a specific routine you follow every morning?

Angel: My morning routine consists of an intense gym workout, typically CrossFit style, then a mental rehearsal visualization that I have used for over ten years: I visualize my day unfolding, getting everything I want done with an abundance of energy and focus, then I rewind it, fast-forward it, and rewind it again. It takes less than five minutes and can be heightened with music. I will anchor these feelings with the snap of my fingers, so I can bring them back when I need them most, such as prior to stepping out onstage to deliver a speech. This practice tricks your brain into thinking you have been there and done it before, hence any anxiety or overwhelming thoughts about your upcoming projects or the day ahead quickly disappear. I follow this up with a light breakfast (or no breakfast) and wait until lunch to eat. I also occasionally follow an intermittent fasting protocol to help with focus and energy.

Entrepreneur: What are some things you learned from the advances in neuroscience and biohacking?

Angel: I learned to look at the same problem, but ask a very different question about it than you usually do. Take, for example, the idea of finding willpower. To have willpower is, by definition, to apply self-control, which implies that something within yourself must be out of control. So what is that? After speaking with biohackers, neuroscientists, doctors, and a clinical social worker, I discovered that the need for willpower increases significantly when our energy levels decrease. With this drop, a decline in cognitive abilities kicks in, such as decision fatigue and an inability to focus and concentrate. Willpower exists to help us push through this cognitive decline.

It is also precisely at this point that we shift into self-preservation mode. Sensing depleted energy, our brain switches gears to reserve the remaining energy supply for vital bodily functions—and reaching your goals or resisting cravings isn't one of them. So what happens is this: 1) Your brain fails to adequately assess the consequences of our decisions, (e.g., you eat an entire pizza) or, 2) Your brain does nothing.

Willpower is an internal fight that pits you against yourself. When we understand that willpower is a symptom and not a cause, we can uncover why it occurs: low energy. By closing the energy gap—the distance between the energy you have and the energy required to reach your goals—you see that willpower is only needed in emergency situations. In a study of 2,500 entrepreneurs internationally, we found that 90 percent of those who felt they did not have the stamina to achieve their goals experience brain fog. This requires them to use more willpower, as they not only have to fight against very real cognitive declines, but they also have to manage the status quo of their daily lives. Forget any goals they want to achieve—there isn't enough energy to focus on those, too. This was a staggering revelation to me. By addressing low energy and brain fog, you immediately increase an individual's ability to focus, concentrate, remember, and get into the "zone" where everything flows naturally. You also give them a surplus of energy to help them troubleshoot major issues, instigate change, and focus on their passions.

Next time you observe yourself struggling to do something you don't want to do, ask this question: Is my energy low? Fix that first and everything else will fall into place because you'll switch back on your ability to focus and manage your time and energy effectively. Any time you find yourself "efforting" is an indication something is out of alignment. Find out what that is, and you'll unlock potential you've never experienced before.

Entrepreneur: You have spent a lot of time with supersuccessful people. What are some of the common habits they all share?

Angel: One of the biggest realizations I've had in recent times is that what they do may influence my habits, but it never provides me with the full picture. Delving into biohacking, I started asking the question: What would happen, for example, if I depleted a peak performer of something as basic as their vitamin D? They would potentially go into a deep depression and end up curled up in the fetal position in the corner. They would go from being an active extrovert to an introvert and would want to cut off social contact. Their brain simply wouldn't have the energy required to process the psychological requirements their goals ask of them.

We are each biochemically different and have varying thresholds for stress and change. Why? The supersuccessful have either by accident become biohackers that have given them the perfect biochemistry to work at a high level, or they have hacked it purposefully. Applying a habit of the supersuccessful without having hacked your own biochemistry to enhance your brain function, mood, and focus is about as useful as washing windows on the *Titanic*. It's going to sink if it doesn't have the right environment to float it. Don't get me wrong. You may become supersuccessful by following their strategies, but understand, there's a big difference between being successful and happy and well. In my research, I've found that medications, food sensitivities, disruptions in the microbiome (our healthy gut flora), environmental toxins, and the drop-in nutrition in our food supply all have the ability to derail our mood and our behavior, thereby making change harder.

Attempting to apply a habit of the supersuccessful without addressing these issues will only result in a "ten steps forward, eight steps back" approach, and you'll be left wondering why it didn't work for you. It's the difference between driving on an open freeway with no other cars on the road or getting stuck in peak-hour traffic. Clear the freeway by addressing any nutritional deficiencies that may result in a lack of focus, poor attitude, or even depression; then focus on what the big guns are doing.

Surprisingly, the first place I would begin is by balancing my gut bacteria. The research coming out connecting the microbiome and our mental health is staggering. Some predict depression will be treated via probiotics in the future on a large scale. I now eat for my microbiome because I know how much it impacts cognition, mood, and regulates my energy. This is a crucial first step to take for any individual looking to achieve at a high level. Understand, you cannot perform at a high psychological level without paying a high biological price. Our new environment constantly places us under a consistent level of stress. This comes at the cost of our mood and behavior, not simply a lack of willpower.

PART I
HABITS THAT INCREASE PRODUCTIVITY—REFLECTIONS

While old habits may die hard, new habits can give new life to success. Neuroscience has shown that when we introduce certain habits into our daily lives, we rewire and condition our brains to achieve our goals. This can be as simple as repeating very specific and positive affirmations about ourselves or carving out 15 minutes each day to master a new skill.

In order to understand what influences our behavior, scientists have studied how and why we form certain habits. They've narrowed it down to a habit loop that occurs in three steps: cue, routine, reward. A cue triggers a habit (for example, picking up your phone causes you to check Instagram, or listening to a certain playlist makes you feel more creative). The routine is the behavior itself. The reward is what happens when your brain responds positively to the habit. A nice shot of dopamine washes over your brain that helps it remember the habit loop. And the cycle continues: cue, routine, reward.

Science also tells us which habits increase our productivity and which stop us in our tracks. The bad news: Some of the habits you thought were helping you—like packing your schedule with back-to-back meetings or multitasking—are actually limiting your productivity. The good news: Old habits can be changed and replaced with new habits that really will benefit you. By simply identifying the habits that hold us back and the habits that propel us forward, science is doing a lot of the work for us right out of the gate.

IMPRESSIONS THAT CLOSE DEALS

There's a famous maxim, sometimes attributed to Oscar Wilde and sometimes to Will Rogers, that says, "You never get a second chance to make a good first impression." While this might seem like a slight exaggeration, studies show that impressions really do matter. Researchers at Princeton

University found that all it took was a tenth of a second to form an impression of a stranger from their face. What's more, longer exposures didn't significantly change those impressions.

From the quality of your LinkedIn profile photo to the UX of your website, the representation of yourself or your brand means everything.

Lucky for us, researchers are beginning to identify the factors that make both good and bad impressions in business. Some of the secret sauce rests in your outward physical appearance: the way you smile (or don't), the way you dress, or your body language. These may seem like superficial things, but how you come across visually to others is important. It can be the difference between being memorable or being forgettable, or—even worse—being unlikable.

Impressions can also be fostered through your behavior. Entrepreneurs who take a personal approach to their customers have been shown to be more effective than those who are more hands off. Employees who listen more than they talk also leave a much more positive impression. In the chapters that follow, you'll see research on everything from where to sit in a bar if you want to close a deal to the emojis you shouldn't use if you want to be taken seriously in the workplace (hint: all of them).

Then there are the intangibles that universally attract people and make them want to do business with you. These can be things like the "familiarity principle," a psychological phenomenon that causes people to prefer products they are more familiar with. Trust is another big factor. Studies have shown that people are willing to pay a premium for products and services that they have faith in. Meanwhile, they're much more likely to drop a company that has broken their trust.

For all the research on making good impressions, there's an equal amount of information on what *not* to do. Some of it might seem obvious, such as not lying. But other findings may surprise you. For example, one study showed that something as simple as a bad LinkedIn photo can affect the impression you make as fast as a hummingbird flaps its wings, while another study found that people who slouch are more likely to have low self-confidence.

While scientists continue to study the effect that both good and bad impressions have on success, one finding can't be ignored: Making a lasting impression sets a powerful tone that is difficult to reverse. As Carl W. Buehner once said, "They may forget what you said, but they will never forget how you made them feel."

In the following chapters, you will be introduced to a variety of scientifically backed strategies, such as body language pointers and behavior tweaks, that will both make you feel good about yourself and make others feel good about you.

FIVE RESEARCH-BACKED STRATEGIES TO INCREASE YOUR SALES REVENUES

John Stevens

Without awareness and traffic, your website will never be able to convert customers. On the other hand, most businesses put too *much* emphasis on generating traffic and invest insufficiently in optimizing their websites for conversion.

According to research from Eisenberg Holdings, for every $92 that the average company spends to attract visitors, it spends just $1 to convert them. This explains the abysmal conversion rates many companies suffer from (with rates typically under 3.5 percent, according to Monetate's "Ecommerce Quarterly Report"). It also explains why generating revenue and staying profitable are among the most pressing challenges that businesses face today.

Thankfully, your business *can* be made more profitable. Ample research has been conducted on what it takes to bring your company out of the red and into the black. Here are five research-backed principles guaranteed to hike your revenue.

1. Smart, Personalized Email Marketing

Research shows that email is the most effective of all marketing channels—both inbound and outbound. Data from the Direct Marketing Association shows that you can expect an ROI of $38 from every $1 spent on email marketing. And research by Monetate, which analyzed more than 500 million shopping experiences, found that email (at 3.19 percent) beats search (1.95 percent) and social media (0.71 percent) combined when it comes to driving sales.

If you haven't invested in segmented or triggered email marketing already, it's time to start, since doing so could double your revenue. Once you've gotten started with email, take things a step further by fully personalizing your messages. According to MarketingSherpa, simply personalizing your emails can boost your sales by up to 208 percent over using the general "batch-and-blast" email approach.

2. Upselling and Cross Selling

Extensive research has shown that upselling and cross selling are two of the most effective ways to boost revenue in a business. At one point, Amazon attributed up to 35 percent of its revenue to cross selling, and JetBlue was able to generate $190 million in additional revenue in 2014 simply by upselling its users. According to social ecommerce platform Viralstyle, simply enabling upsells can "automatically increase your average profit by an additional 15 to 25 percent."

The two challenges involved with upsells and cross sells are relevance and timing. Make sure that your content-management system is capable of associating related products. That way, when you offer an upgrade or a multi-item bundle, that move will make sense, given your site visitors' browsing patterns.

Also, to ensure that your offer doesn't turn off a prospect who would otherwise become a converted customer, consider setting it to appear as part of the checkout experience instead of as a suggestion on a product page.

3. Increase Your Trust Factor

Trust plays a major role in the average customer's decision to buy from you, and unless you can effectively optimize and increase your trust factor, your business will basically be leaving money on the table.

Earning Your Customers' Trust

While there are many ways to amplify your company's impression of trustworthiness—and, ultimately, every tip in this chapter will help you do that in some way—here are some of the most effective ways:

- *Use security seals.* Research shows that displaying security seals on your website (such as SiteLock, PayPal Verified, or Norton Secured) is the foremost way to get people to trust and buy from you. Simply embedding a familiar security seal will go a long way to increase your trust factor and maximize sales.
- *Enable SSL.* Enabling SSL (Secure Sockets Layer) technology, which creates an encrypted link between your site and the customer's browser, can massively boost sales; when

people see the green padlock and "HTTPS" in their browser's address bar, they're more likely to buy from you.

- *Make an address and phone number visible.* Available data shows that having a visible phone number and physical address on your website can boost sales by up to 5 percent.
- *Have a social media presence.* Even if you're a brick and mortar store, you'll lose out on a lot of business if you don't have a diverse digital footprint. In addition to your website, you should maintain an active, attentive presence on each of the major social networks.

4. Opt for a Faster Website

How much do you think each one-second delay in site loading time costs ecommerce giant Amazon? Try a massive $1.6 billion annually. Yes, every single year! And it's not just Amazon. It's been estimated that a one-second delay in any site's load time will result in a 7 percent loss in conversions.

People simply don't have the patience to watch web pages slowly render in today's "everything on demand" climate. Slow websites cost the U.S. ecommerce industry as a whole around $500 billion annually.

Simply making your website faster can—and will—boost sales dramatically. According to data from Gomez, which monitored real user data from 33 major retailers, decreasing page load time from eight to two seconds increases conversion rates by a whopping 74 percent.

5. Leverage the Authority of Social Proof

The key to boosting sales lies in using this psychological phenomenon as a form of social proof: Simply having someone respected as an authority in your niche endorse your product can double or triple sales. Just ask Weight Watchers.

When Oprah Winfrey announced that she had invested in the company, a form of authority endorsement, its stock prices shot up by 110 percent overnight. If you are struggling to convert sales and generate revenue, consider sponsoring a relevant industry authority—or influencer—to endorse your brand.

As the studies referenced here show, increasing your business revenue by 30 percent, 50 percent, 100 percent, or even more is certainly within reach. Leverage the above principles in your business, and watch your revenue and profit skyrocket.

FIVE RESEARCH-BACKED TIPS TO INCREASE ONLINE SALES

John Stevens

Sixty-three percent of people requesting information about your company today won't purchase from you for at least three months, and 20 percent won't purchase over the next 12 months. Another disheartening statistic—44 percent of salespeople have an 80 percent probability that they won't close the sale.

While many factors influence whether prospects will buy from you, most can be traced back to psychology. Extensive research has been conducted to learn what really makes people buy. This chapter shares five research-backed tips for boosting your online sales.

1. Get an Authority Figure to Endorse You

How much is an endorsement from Oprah Winfrey worth to your business? For T-fal ActiFry, it was worth $150 million. On February 15, 2013, Oprah tweeted and posted on Instagram—while holding an ActiFry—that the low-fat cooker "changed my life." Analysts estimated the resulting increase in share value was worth more than $150 million.

Almost every big brand can testify to the power of an endorsement from an authority figure, and it explains why all major brands try to sign celebrities and athletes to endorse them—Nike, Weight Watchers, Coca-Cola, etc.

Having an authority figure—especially one who is well-respected in your field—endorse your products will go a long way toward boosting your sales. In the absence of an authority figure, having a respected media outlet endorse you can have the same effect.

2. Leverage the Power of the Crowd

There's a popular saying, attributed to P.T. Barnum, that nothing attracts a crowd like a crowd. Research shows this saying is true. In a famous 1951 experiment by psychologist Solomon Asch to observe how people make decisions in a group, he found that people are more likely to bury their views, even if they are correct, and embrace that of the group.

Social proof is one of the most effective tools for boosting sales. If you can get people to see that many others like them are happily using your product or service, you will be able to easily and successfully boost product sales.

3. Leverage the Familiarity Principle

Have you ever wondered why brands keep repeating the same ads across different channels, or sometimes again and again on the same channel? A quick experiment conducted by Charles Goetzinger in 1968 gives some insight into how the familiarity principle works. He had a student repeatedly come to his class at Oregon State University completely enclosed in a large black bag, with only his feet showing. The other students in the class at first reacted with dislike, then with curiosity, and finally with acceptance. He concluded repeated exposure can make us develop a liking for something we initially hated.

The reason for the students' eventual friendship toward the black bag is also the reason why major brands keep repeating the same ad again and again—which research shows works, by the way. It's due to the "mere-exposure effect" or the "familiarity principle," which is a psychological phenomenon that states that people tend to develop a preference for things they are familiar with.

There's also a marketing rule dedicated to this—called "the rule of seven"—which basically states that your prospects need to be exposed to your offer at least seven times before taking note of it and taking action.

So don't hesitate to repeatedly let people know about your offer. Tell them through every available channel, repeatedly, and watch your sales go through the roof. Use social media, build an email list, use advertising, start a blog, leverage offline events, and use any other means necessary.

4. Boost Sales by Increasing Your Site Speed

In a study monitoring real user data from 33 major retailers, it was discovered that reducing page load time from eight to two seconds can boost conversion rates by 74 percent. It was also observed that a one-second delay in site loading time reduces conversion by 7 percent.

With all the right sales measures in place, speed of access is important. There are so many things going on in the mind of prospects, and a 2015 Microsoft study shows that our attention span has declined from 12 seconds in the year 2000 to eight. People are simply too impatient to wait for an ever-loading website.

Work on making your website faster, especially transaction pages, and you'll be amazed at the resulting increase in sales.

5. Improve Your Trust Factor

Sales hinge on trust, but in an internet age that is rife with hacks and scams, trust is more important than ever. Research shows that as many as 48 percent of people don't feel comfortable transacting with a site that does not have a trust seal. Trust seals are the highest trust signal people look for when performing transactions on a website, and 48 percent of people won't buy from you if they are not in place.

Just as important is to have SSL enabled. When making online transactions, people pay special attention to the HTTPS protocol, and having that green padlock displayed alongside your site URL can go a long way toward boosting your sales. It has been observed that having SSL enabled can boost sales by 30 percent or more.

If you don't use SSL on your site, you're still leaving doubts in your prospects' minds. Enabling SSL will help you seem more reliable to your prospective customers.

SCIENCE WARNS DON'T DO THESE SIX THINGS IF YOU WANT TO GET HIRED

John Boitnott

After months of looking, you've finally landed an interview for your dream job. If all goes well, this could put an end to your job search for years. You've submitted your resume and studied the most likely interview questions, but are you really prepared?

Even with all your preparation and experience, one mistake could lead the hirer to choose someone else for the position. It's important to know what those mistakes could be so you can avoid them. Here are some common interview slip-ups, backed by science, that could cost you your dream job.

1. Talk Instead of Listen

Studies have revealed that people spend 60 percent of a conversation talking about themselves. Even in an interview, the ideal conversation is a give-and-take, with the candidate waiting for cues before speaking. If you're the type who tends to chatter uncontrollably when you're nervous, take a deep breath and listen. You don't need to dominate the conversation. Let the important person interviewing you do that. Try to stay on track when you're speaking and avoid sharing more than your interviewer wants to know.

2. Lie

People aren't as skilled at detecting a lie as you might think. Although there are body language cues that someone might be deceptive, those can be unreliable. The biggest giveaway that someone is lying is in the words themselves. If you start to tell an untrue story, chances are fairly decent you'll slip and contradict yourself. Even if you manage not to, the interviewer may detect that something doesn't sound right in your answer and mark you off the list of potential hires. The best course of action is to answer questions as truthfully as possible.

3. Show Up Dressed for Yard Work

The outfit you choose the morning of an interview could have everything to do with whether you land the job. When surveyed, 72 percent of hiring managers said that dressing inappropriately is one of the biggest mistakes an applicant can make. Leave the jeans and T-shirts at home and invest in clothing that makes you look professional, even if the dress code of the business in question is somewhat casual. Also avoid tight or revealing clothing that comes across as provocative. Managers tend to respond more favorably to neutral colors like black and navy blue rather than bright colors or distracting accessories.

4. Wing It

Studies have found that employees who are passionate about their employers and the work they do are happier and more productive. However, many job searchers end up settling for a company they know little about. Before you apply for an opening, take time to research the company and determine whether you can get excited about it. You can use Glassdoor to learn what they're like as an employer, but you can also research their products and community outreach to see if you share the same core values. Once you do land an interview, conduct extensive research into the company so you'll be able to answer questions knowledgeably.

5. Accept the First Low Salary Offered

It can be tempting, especially if you've been out of work for a while, to accept an initial offer at the low end of the range. But by doing this, you may be cheating yourself out of thousands of dollars each year. Research shows that employers respond better during salary negotiations to precise counteroffers. Not only are you more likely to get more money in your bank account, but your employer may also have more respect for you if you can ask for what you want and get it.

6. Do Nothing After the Interview

After the interview, many candidates choose to sit by the phone and wait for it to ring, yet follow-ups are an important part of landing a job. If an employer is on the fence, that extra email could make all the difference. Research finds that if you're going to get a response to your follow-up email, it will be within 24 to 48 hours of sending it. However, if you don't hear back, it still isn't time to rest. You have a 21 percent chance of getting a reply on a second email and a 25 percent chance of getting a reply if you continue to follow up.

Finding a job can be stressful, but science can help you make decisions that up your chances of winning an interview. As a result of careful advance research and preparation, you can find the perfect fit on your first try. This will not only make the job search easier, but it may also reduce your risk of going through the process again in a couple of years.

FIVE STEPS TO GETTING YOUR BRAND "HIRED" IN THE REAL WORLD

Taddy Hall and Linda Deeken

If you're like most people, you probably assumed that this chapter would be talking about humans, not brands. After all, who has even considered the notion of brands getting "hired" for a job?

Yet that lapse is a large part of the problem plaguing the growth trajectories of many brands in the consumer packaged goods space today.

In reality, consumers don't simply buy products or services; they *hire* them to do a job, or to enact progress in their lives. From purchases as large as a home to as trivial as a chocolate bar, consumers are constantly hiring (or "firing") brands. As this chapter's co-author Taddy Hall uncovered in the book he co-wrote, *Competing Against Luck*, the missing link in most innovation approaches is consumers' needs, which in this context we'll call "jobs."

Put differently, what separates innovation success from innovation failure is a company's ability to align with a consumer job.

Let's begin with some definitions. A Job (capitalized here to help make our point) is the progress that a person is trying to make in a particular circumstance. A Job meets four key criteria: First, a Job helps a person achieve a goal or aspiration. It is a process by which he or she makes progress.

Second, a Job has context within the daily flow of life. A successful solution can only be created relative to a specific context or circumstance. Third, and most critically, a Job has important social and emotional dimensions, which can be more powerful than its outward function. Finally, a Job is ongoing and recurring.

Within that context, how well do you understand the Job or Jobs for which your products are currently being hired? Equally important, how well do you understand the Jobs for which your products "aspire" to be hired? What separates your brand's resume from the resume of the "ideal" brand competing for the same Job?

Analyzing consumer Jobs, or jobs theory, is a strategy employed by the world's fastest-growing and most-respected companies, such as Anheuser-Busch, Kraft, and Nestlé. Jobs theory describes the notion that consumers effectively hire brands and products in order to make progress in their lives.

When applied correctly, the jobs theory can revolutionize a company's ratio of innovation success.

Consider, for example, OnStar. Left to their own devices, OnStar's team members could have compiled an endless list of services for which consumers could hire them. The problem was, that laundry list was too confusing. What consumers really wanted was peace of mind, and OnStar needed to align against that Job.

So what are the steps a brand should take to align with jobs theory? There are five:

Step 1: Find a Job

Look for Jobs you can fill by reflecting on your personal experiences. Find people who aren't using your product, or consider what tasks people don't want to do. Your consumers can provide inspiration as they come up with their own work-arounds.

Purina, for example, found that consumers actually stored clean litter in the trunks of their cars and replenished their litter boxes from there until the boxes were light enough to bring indoors. This was a clear Job the company could solve with new Tidy Cats LightWeight.

To find a Job, ask:

- What progress are your consumers trying to achieve?
- What are the circumstances of their struggle?
- What obstacles are getting in the way of your consumers making that progress?
- Are your consumers compromising with imperfect solutions?
- How would your consumers define the "quality" of a better solution, and what trade-offs are they willing to make?

Step 2: Solve the Job

Once the Job is clear, solving it in a manner that's beneficial for consumers and company alike is key. The Tidy Cats team exemplified this rule, asserting that its task had never been "about achieving acceptable minimums." Instead, "We were focused on maximizing the opportunity," according to brand director Rebecca Schulz, quoted in the Nielsen 2015

"Breakthrough Innovation Report." The team worked to deliver on the promise of uncompromising litter performance at half the weight—and deliver they did.

To achieve this:

- Outline what your consumers want to accomplish from a functional, emotional, and social perspective.
- List the trade-offs the consumers are willing to make.
- Make yourself the preferred solution, even if the Job is already getting done. List competing solutions and other obstacles.

Step 3: Get Hired

Tell consumers why they should hire you. For Tidy Cats, "feeling was believing," so the Tidy Cats team offered in-store lift tests during its product launch, proving its lightweight benefit to consumers in a tangible way.

Why should consumers change? Two strategies to use:

1. Share the "push" of the unsatisfied Job and the "pull" of the new solution.
2. Address the forces inhibiting change, such as anxieties about a new solution.

Step 4: Organize Around the Job and Reap the Benefits

Focusing on a clearly defined consumer Job yields four key benefits:

1. *Distributed decision making.* Employees throughout the organization are empowered to make decisions that align with the Job, and to be autonomous and innovative.

2. *Resource optimization.* When an organization is focused on getting hired for a consumer Job, it can better prioritize resources around solving that Job. If any resources aren't being spent toward solving the Job, they can be rebalanced accordingly.

3. *Inspiration.* Solving a consumer's Job is inherently inspiring to individuals in an organization, enabling them to see their work making progress in people's lives.

4. *Better measurement.* With a focus on the Job, people will naturally seek to measure and manage to more consumer-centric metrics.

Step 5: Avoid the Pitfalls

Three fallacies threaten the success of a well-executed Job:

1. *The fallacy of active data.* Growing companies start to generate operations-related data

(active data), which can seduce managers with its apparent objectivity. In fact, this data may be far removed from the true picture of the Job.

2. *The fallacy of surface growth.* As companies invest in consumer relationships, they focus their energies on driving growth by selling additional products or solving a broader set of Jobs—known as surface growth—rather than improving their solution for the core Job.

3. *The fallacy of nonconforming data.* Managers focus on generating data that conforms to pre-existing notions. This inherently blinds managers to emerging opportunities beyond their perspective.

Implement these five simple steps, and you'll be well on your way to improved innovation results. Achieving that improved growth trajectory will come down to the choices you are willing to make.

16

FIVE SCIENTIFIC ELEMENTS OF A GREAT FIRST IMPRESSION

Carolyn Sun

In the business world, a good first impression is crucial. It primes how you're seen and responded to. The reason the first impression is so powerful is because the human brain judges information sequentially, according to Arthur Dobrin, a researcher in the science of first impressions.

"The exaggerated impact of first impressions is related to the halo effect," he says, "that phenomenon whereby the perception of positive qualities in one thing or part gives rise to the perception of similar qualities in related things or in the whole."

You have seven measly seconds (some say less) to exude trustworthiness and competence during a first meeting. Research demonstrates bad first impressions are not only tough to shake, but also have the tendency to create a self-fulfilling feedback loop. In other words, if you make a poor first impression on someone, you'll be on the receiving end of aloof or unfriendly behavior in turn. You are then more likely to reciprocate this aloof behavior, reinforcing the person's initial bad impression. (On the flip side, the same goes for good first impressions.)

There is good news: Because first impressions are so important, there is a rich body of research on what verbal and nonverbal cues go into making a good first impression. While certain elements are simply out of our control—such as the faces we were born with—there are five elements very much within our purview. To nail a good first impression, check out this short list of what to do.

1. Get Your Appearance Right

Your physical appearance and how you dress impact how people judge your character and abilities. Studies by researchers in the United Kingdom and Turkey illustrate that clothing has a massive impact on how we are judged. For instance, in a study where subjects examined images of a man in an off-the-rack suit and the same man in a made-to-measure suit, subjects rated the made-to-measure version significantly higher in confidence, success, flexibility, and income than the off-the-rack version.

Clothing matters, and while you may not be able to afford tailor-made or high-end attire, you may be able to have the clothes you already possess altered and hemmed so they better fit your frame and look sharp.

You can also ensure that you look clean and neat (tuck in your top, keep your hair styled, and, if it applies to you, use simple makeup) and are dressed appropriately for the work or social situation.

Every occupation and office tends to have its own dress code, from Silicon Valley to publishing to finance, and there is no single way to dress for all occasions. It's up to you to crack that code, and one simple way to do so is through imitation. Look at the well-dressed employees and leaders in your field (the ones who aren't known for their eccentric clothes) for cues. Are they wearing suit jackets, or is it more of a vintage T-shirt kind of office?

Also, it never hurts to be prepared for both casual and dressy scenarios: If you can, keep some dress shoes, a dress shirt or blouse, and a dress jacket at work, in case you have to dress up for an unexpected meeting, presentation, or event.

2. Stand With Good Posture

Your posture and body language matter, largely because these nonverbal cues tap into people's primal ability to judge whether someone is friend or foe—or, in today's terms, a person's "trustworthiness," says Amy Cuddy, an expert on body language and author of *Presence*.

Cuddy advises you to carry yourself in a way that is "powerful and proud." One way to do that is to slow down your breathing, pull your shoulders back and down, stand up tall, and firmly plant your feet on the ground. "If you're carrying yourself in a way that's powerful and proud, you're saying to yourself, 'I'm safe. I'm OK. I deserve to be here.' And that is what comes across," she says.

Also keep your shoulders square to the person you're speaking with, so you look as though you're giving him your full attention. And you can always revert to the famous Wonder Woman pose—legs planted slightly apart and hands on your hips.

3. Mind Your Hands

A lot of people don't know what to do with their hands, so pay attention. "Be aware of the power of a handshake," University of Illinois researcher Sanda Dolcos says. "[The handshake] not only increases the positive effect toward a favorable interaction, but it also diminishes the impact of a negative impression. Many of our social interactions may go wrong for one reason or another, and a simple handshake preceding them can give us a boost and attenuate the negative impact of possible misunderstandings."

The recipe for a good handshake is to make it firm, dry (you can apply antiperspirant to your hands), and about two or three seconds long—and accompany it with good eye contact and a smile. Keep in mind that an overly aggressive "death grip" can be just as off-putting as a limp handshake.

What we do with our hands when we talk or listen matters, too. People who gesticulate frequently tend to build trust quicker than those who don't. One reason for this is that our hands enhance our communications and act as a highly visible cue for others to see our intentions and sincerity. However, there's a sweet spot. Keep your hands below the collarbone. "Any higher and you're going to appear frantic," says Alison Craig, image consultant and author of *Hello Job! How to Psych Up, Suit Up, & Show Up*.

Also keep your hands in an area that spans 180 degrees from your navel. "Gesturing from here communicates that you're centered, controlled, and calm—and that you want to help," body language expert Mark Bowden says.

4. Make Eye Contact

Eye contact is meaningful. It can make you appear more honest, more memorable, and more persuasive and establish a stronger connection with whomever you're addressing. But too much of it can come off as confrontational or creepy. Too little, and you appear timid or shifty.

The sweet spot is to look someone in the eye 60 to 70 percent of the time you're interacting with them, according to communication and body language experts Barbara and Allan Pease. For those who find eye contact challenging, you can always try the old "look at the eyebrows or the space between the eyes" trick. That is, until you get more confident with eye contact.

Also be mindful of blinking too much or rubbing your eyes when you first meet someone. When people are nervous, they tend to blink more than usual, body language expert Lillian Glass says: "Your nerves are firing rapidly, your subconscious is working overtime, and your eyes dry up to compensate." Regardless of why, the effect can be off-putting.

5. Demonstrate Trustworthiness

Because establishing your trustworthiness is the single most important part of creating a good first impression, your entire attitude—how you behave and hold yourself—needs to demonstrate that you can be trusted. That means that when you're talking to someone, stand (or sit) straight or lean in, but don't lean back, and keep your hands out of your pockets. You want your body language to demonstrate that you're comfortable and want to be there.

While in conversation, let the person or people you're talking to lead. You can establish trustworthiness by actively listening. People feel trust when they feel listened to and understood, according to Travis Bradberry, co-author of *Emotional Intelligence 2.0*. Make sure you have some active listening prompts ("I'd love to hear more about that") and questions ("What is your biggest takeaway from that experience?") to help the conversation along and show that you're actively listening and not working off some generic script.

As you listen, be mindful not to fidget, as in shaking your legs, tapping your fingers, or checking your phone. All these actions give the impression that you don't want to be there.

And one last thing: smile. It is such an easy, graceful way to put someone else at ease, and there are few things more off-putting than having to talk to an unsmiling sourpuss.

CLOSING A DEAL AT A RESTAURANT? THIS RESEARCH CAN HELP

Jeffery Lindenmuth

We close deals in bars and restaurants to relax, get away from our routines, and make toasting our next success a little easier. But if you are meeting at a bar, choose your location carefully. Research shows control is key, and where you sit could make or break a deal.

Avoid the Doors and Windows

Researchers find that when we're warmer, we're more likely to judge people as trustworthy and act more generously. In other words, feeling physically warm makes us emotionally warm, too. Case in point: The study found that people who held a hot drink were 11 percent more likely to rate the person they were talking to as warm than those holding a cold one. In another study, those who were warm were more likely to choose a gift for others than for themselves. So order that cup of tea, coffee, or hot cider. And sit as far away as possible from drafty doorways or windows.

Pick a Smooth Table

For a study in the journal *Social Cognitive and Affective Neuroscience*, participants touched rough or smooth surfaces before judging social interactions. Those who'd touched rough ones viewed others as more difficult and adversarial.

Take the Hard Seat

When researchers from Harvard, MIT, and Yale asked people to haggle over the price of a car, participants who were parked in hard, wooden chairs were tougher negotiators than those seated in soft, cushioned chairs. They changed their offer prices less over the course of the negotiation, offering 28 percent less than people in soft chairs. This suggests that when people come into contact with soft products, they may be easier to negotiate with. Take the hard seat and use its rigidity in your favor.

Put Your Phone Away

It takes the average brain just 200 milliseconds to determine a person's emotional state based on facial expressions, according to research from the University of Glasgow's Centre for Cognitive Neuroimaging. The study showed that the brain starts by looking at the eyes, zooms out to process the whole face, and then closes back in to examine specifics, such as a smiling mouth. So if you want to make a good impression, be sure to look up at the person across from you, not down at Candy Crush on your phone.

No Slouching

People with strong posture are more likely than their hunchbacked counterparts to feel good about themselves, according to an Ohio State University study. So sit up straight (and avoid a low table), and have the confidence to seal that deal.

EIGHT SCIENCE-BACKED TECHNIQUES THAT WILL MAKE YOU MORE LIKABLE

Stephen J. Bronner

We all want to be liked. After all, likable people have more friends, are more respected by their employees and co-workers, and close more deals.

While you can't force or trick someone into liking you, you can make yourself more emotionally appealing to people. As Michelle Tillis Lederman, author of *The 11 Laws of Likability* and *Nail the Interview, Land the Job*, puts it, "You can't make anybody like you, but you can enable people to see what is likable about you. A lot of these things are not necessarily tricks that are meant to manipulate and deceive, but they're honest ways we connect and make others feel good."

Jack Schafer, a behavioral analyst, retired FBI agent, and author of *The Like Switch*, says that good salespeople do these things instinctively, which is what makes them so successful.

"It's little things that get people to like you," he says. "You have to pay attention to those things."

Here are eight science-backed techniques you can start employing immediately to make yourself a more appealing person:

1. Smile

If it sounds simple, that's because it is. Smiling triggers your brain to release endorphins, which makes you feel good. And guess what? Smiling is contagious.

"People read your body language and facial expressions far more than hear your words or hear your tone of voice," Lederman says, "so that smile is immediately welcoming, disarming, and relaxing to the other person."

You shouldn't just smile at everyone, though, says Tim Sanders, author of *The Likeability Factor*. It has to come from a place of authenticity. However, you should always smile back at someone who is smiling at you.

"When you smile back at someone, what you are combining is friendliness and authenticity together," he says. "Often, when we don't expect a person to smile at us or we don't know them very well, we look away. When you smile back at a person, you're telling them, 'I like you, too,' and that generates more likability."

2. Watch Your Body Language

We humans are just animals in fancy clothes. That's why, along with smiling, you can use visual cues to let other people know you're not a threat. These include raising your eyebrows and tilting your head, Schafer says. The head tilt exposes your vital carotid artery to the other person, showing trust. Crazy, right?

"What typically happens is our brains are looking for threats in the environment," he says. "We communicate nonverbally. When the brain sees friendly signals, it can focus on other things. It's important to learn about these signals so we can use them appropriately."

Stressful situations, such as job interviews or client meetings, trigger your flight-or-fight response, making you closed off and defensive. Intentionally using these physical signals, along with smiling, can override this heightened state.

3. Make the Other Person Feel Good

"If you want people to like you, make them feel good about themselves," Schafer says. "We have to take the focus off us and put it onto the other person."

There are many ways to accomplish this. "Appreciation, recognition, a thank-you, direct eye contact, a compliment, asking their advice—all of these are ways in which we make someone feel good," Lederman says.

In conversations, employ empathic statements. For example, Schafer suggests, if someone looks happy, say something like, "Looks like you're having a good day." If she responds, "I just closed a deal," you can reply, "You must have worked hard." She will walk away feeling good, and those feelings will reflect on you. But avoid direct flattery, as that can make people defensive.

4. Be Engaged

Why are Bill Clinton, Oprah Winfrey, and Ellen DeGeneres so likable? All three know how to make others feel like the most important people in the world when talking with them. There are some simple ways to follow their example:

"Leave your phone at your desk. If you have a meeting, turn it off and turn it over," Sanders says. "Look that person straight in the eye and be fully engaged the entire conversation. If you're at lunch, don't pay attention to anyone else around you but your server."

Even be aware of details such as where your cups are placed, Schafer says. If they are between you and the other person, they can act as a barrier. Make sure they're off to the side.

5. Be Engaging

Remember, people love to talk about themselves, and when they're having a good time, they'll feel good about you, too.

Open conversations with someone by asking about his "wow project"—something he is working on and really excited about, Sanders says. "Listen until they're tired of talking about their passion project. Usually, it's five minutes, but it will be the best five minutes of that conversation."

You should also be thoughtful about the follow-up questions you ask. "Ask a question in an open-ended format that shows you're really interested in the answer," Lederman says. "From that point, you can listen and ask additional questions, probe a little further—don't interrogate—or you can listen and share. When you share something of yourself on the same topic, you start to show a connection, a relatability, a commonality, and people like people like them."

Finding common ground is a classic technique to build rapport. You can do this by finding things you have in common with the other person, building a relationship over time, or, most powerfully, through a third person, such as a common connection or a close friend who works in the same industry as your conversation partner.

6. Show Up

You're more likely to like those with whom you are familiar, such as co-workers, neighbors, or that person you always run into at the gym.

"The mere-exposure effect is about familiarity, and that just means showing up," says Theo Tsaousides, a neuropsychologist, speaker, and author of *Brainblocks: Overcoming the 7 Hidden Barriers to Success*.

Persistence is key here, but obviously don't cross the line into stalking. For example, Tsaousides says frequenting the same cafe, sending emails, and posting and/or commenting on a person's social media accounts are some good tactics to try.

"It's a reminder that you're thinking of them," he says.

7. Adopt a Giving Philosophy

This is the concept that Lederman says increases all results. Whenever you meet someone, you should always be thinking about how you can help him. It won't always pay off immediately, but this philosophy has a cascading effect.

"Giving creates value. To apply the law of giving is to think about how you add value to others," Lederman says. "When you're in a business situation, your thinking is not 'How do I get the deal and what I need out of this customer?' but 'How am I adding value to this customer?'"

Sanders has a simple way to accomplish this goal: During every conversation, you should strive to give a piece of advice, he says. That will separate you from everyone else and make you more likable.

"When you're sending messages to someone that 'I care enough to help you,' you're giving that person a message of 'I'm worthy to continue this relationship,'" Lederman says.

8. Validate People's Opinions

You don't have to agree with everyone, but you should go out of your way to make sure that every person feels she has been heard. Treat feelings as facts, Sanders says. For example, if a customer complains, seriously consider the feedback and let him or her know that it will be discussed internally.

"Psychologists would say that when you accept another person's feelings and you learn to say, 'I'm sorry, I can only imagine how you feel,'" Sanders says, "you deliver to them a powerful psychological benefit called 'validation' that they're not alone or stupid for feeling that way."

Lederman agrees. "What validation really does is give a sense of empowerment," she says. "It tells how that response or thought had an impact, whether or not it's agreed with."

SCIENCE JUST GAVE US ANOTHER REASON NOT TO USE EMOJIS AT WORK

Nina Zipkin

So much of our communication at work is text-based, but sometimes nuance can get lost. It's tempting to drop in an emoji to make sure a response doesn't seem too harsh, but there's a good reason to hold off on that smiley face.

A 2017 study from Ben-Gurion University, the University of Haifa, and the University of Amsterdam found that using smiley emojis in your email correspondence could give a bad impression.

The researchers polled 549 people from 29 countries and had them read work emails from a stranger. They were then asked to rate the competence level and overall warmth of the sender, whose photo was also included.

When a photo of a smiling person was included, the participants perceived the sender of the email as more competent and friendly. But when the correspondence included a smiley emoji, the sender was viewed as less competent, especially when the message related to formal work matters.

The researchers found that when the study participants responded to the formal emails they were given, if the message they were sent included a smiley emoji, their answers had less content and were less detailed.

Additionally, the participants were more likely to assume that the emails with emojis were written by women, although that perception didn't influence how they perceived the sender's competence or friendliness.

In our own informal survey of professionals, we found that using emojis in work email was almost universally shunned. Says Alex Slater, CEO and founder of PR firm the Clyde Group, "I'm a serial emoji user in my personal communications. But at work, it's a hard no. If I receive an emoji from an employee or potential recruit, they might as well include a spelling or grammatical error." Adds Sarah Johnson, a public relations specialist, "Using emojis in a work email is the equivalent of saying, 'Hey, dude.' Even if you know the person on the other end, your email may get forwarded to people you don't know, leaving a bad impression of you."

So if you are trying to make a good first impression, leave the emoji out of your correspondence.

"People tend to assume that a smiley is a virtual smile, but the findings of this study show that in the case of the workplace, at least as far as initial 'encounters' are concerned, this is incorrect," the researchers wrote. "For now, at least, a smiley can only replace a smile when you already know the other person. In initial interactions, it is better to avoid using smileys, regardless of age or gender."

ENTREPRENEUR VOICES SPOTLIGHT: INTERVIEW WITH CHRIS WESTFALL

U.S. National Elevator Pitch Champion

Chris Westfall is the Prince of the Pitch. The U.S. National Elevator Pitch Champion. He's coached clients on *Shark Tank*, helped entrepreneurs raise millions from investors, and rebranded companies with profitable results. He's also the producer and co-host of *The 118 Pitch Course* with Bloomberg TV's Jeffrey Hayzlett and the author of two bestselling books, *The New Elevator Pitch* and *BulletProof Branding*.

Chris talks to us about how he got into the pitching game, why a good pitch can elevate your brand or services to unimaginable heights, and some of the science and strategies behind crafting a perfect pitch.

Entrepreneur: How did you come up with the idea to devote your career to the art of pitching?

Westfall: I was involved with coaching business clients on a variety of topics, mostly related to career advancement.

That coaching included working on elevator pitches. So I decided to enter an online contest [the U.S. National Elevator Pitch Competition] to see who had the best two-minute speech in the United States. I created a video (on my front porch, no less) and started gaining votes on social media. The contest featured entrepreneurs and academics, business leaders and executives, from all over the country. I had no expectations of the outcome. I tried my best, of course, but I really didn't plan to win. The experience was worthwhile, regardless of the outcome. I was glad I took the journey. It was the destination that surprised me.

That surprise was my "aha" moment, for a couple of reasons. One is that it showed me the value of taking a journey, regardless of the ultimate destination. In other words, playing the game to win, but enjoying myself, no matter what the outcome. Secondly, I had a realization that has followed me my entire life: I had others who saw something in me that I couldn't see for myself. I didn't walk into the competition "thinking like a champion." In fact, I wasn't thinking about anything except creating a great video and doing what I could to move forward in the voting. I focused on the task at hand, rather than seeking a label or recognition or anything like that. That approach (staying in the game and trying to enjoy the ups and downs along the way) describes my life when I am at my best. Some days are better than others, but detaching from labels and outcomes always leads to an "aha!" moment for me (and also for all of my clients!). A national recognition or important victory is a lot like a college graduation: Everyone is offering congratulations, but all you can think of is, "Now what the hell am I going to do?" The answer that showed up was: help others to see things in a new way, and say the things that can change the conversation.

Entrepreneur: What's the biggest mistake people make pitching their business?

Westfall: Entrepreneurs can be pretty self-absorbed. Believe me, I know: I'm an entrepreneur as well. Living with technology, or an innovative idea, can create a self-centered focus—after all, your business idea is your baby. Entrepreneurs have a tendency to want to describe how they make the sausage. Unfortunately, no one really cares, unless they get a taste and decide that it's delicious. In my experience, focusing too much on yourself and your idea is actually deadly in a pitch situation.

Entrepreneurs tend to provide a paint-by-numbers pitch because that's what they teach in a lot of business schools and incubators. It goes something like this:

1. Here's the problem.

2. Here's how huge the problem is. (Look at this potential here!)

3. Here's how we will fix it.

4. Here are the projections, featuring a huge upside in Year 3.

5. Thank you for listening. Now we will return to being self-absorbed and obsessed with our ideas.

Take note of the biggest disappointments on *Dragons' Den* and *Shark Tank*: It's always when the entrepreneurs focus too heavily on themselves (paying themselves a salary, missing the service aspects of the business, locking themselves into an unrealistic valuation or outcome ... you get the picture).

Entrepreneur: So what's the fix for this?

Westfall: While the nuances of the pitch can be complex, the simplest way to fix a self-absorbed approach is to start with what your audience is thinking. In this case, your audience is your investor. What is top of mind for the folks you are pitching? And if your answer is, "I don't know," it's time to do your research. It's counterintuitive for the entrepreneurial journey, but an effective pitch focuses first on your audience, not your technology, concept, or service. If you don't know enough about your audience, you haven't earned the right to ask for their money and their investment. For my clients who are headed onto *Shark Tank*, I always ask: "Who's your Shark?" Who is most likely to invest in your idea, and why? Start there, and then see where you can take your ideas next.

Entrepreneur: You've coached some *Shark Tank* contestants. Describe one of your success stories.

Westfall: Emilio and Giselle Cano are the founders of Ranchero Salsa, a chili sauce brand specializing in authentic family recipes from Mexico that use local ingredients. As contestants on *Shark Tank Australia*, they were excited about the possibility of bringing this unique idea to the country. They nailed it with their pitch, and John McGrath, a Shark who made his fortune in real estate, was the investor. After the event, Emilio shared with me that my pitching techniques helped him win the business by helping him focus on "the high concept and by saying something surprising, unexpected, innovative, and counterintuitive." He also shared the importance of "understanding what solution I could bring to the most important person—my listener—meaning what can I do with, through, and for my listener. What will make them ask 'Tell me more?'"

Entrepreneur: What would you recommend in terms of making a good impression digitally?

Westfall: Consider the same strategies that work when you connect personally. Marketers and branding experts will tell you that there are four "P's": product, price, promotion, and place (distribution). But the fifth "P" is the one that's the most important: personalization. Consider your audience, first and foremost, and how you can serve the people that you care about. Whether that's your boss, your shareholders, your customers, or your connections, consistently look to personalize the value that you can create. You can't be all things to all people. But you can create a message that resonates, both online and in person, when you personalize your value proposition. Focus on your audience first, and your results will flow from there.

Entrepreneur: Your book is entitled *The New Elevator Pitch*. What's new about it? How has pitching changed over the years?

Westfall: *The New Elevator Pitch* has become an international bestseller, used by corporations, business leaders, and universities to help create persuasive stories across all industries. Designed as a hold-your-hand book for the persuasive pitch, the book features a simple, step-by-step process for crafting any kind of influential conversation. Loaded with examples, exercises, and links to videos, the book is really a multimedia guide, including a series of scenarios for using the new elevator pitch. Chapters include the "Why Hire Me" pitch, how to pitch to investors, and guidance on networking conversations.

PART II
IMPRESSIONS THAT CLOSE DEALS—REFLECTIONS

Despite the old adage "You can't judge a book by its cover," science is proving that the cover is pretty darn important, and it has more influence on people's perception than we'd like to think. That's why, in business, it's essential to get a handle on what practices, techniques, and behaviors leave a good impression and which ones fall woefully flat. Covers do matter, so make sure yours is the one most likely to fly off the shelves.

Researchers have studied everything from the way we dress to the way we carry ourselves, the way we sell, and the way we close. As a result, they've been able to pinpoint the best practices to follow, so you no longer have to guess. Still dressing like a slacker at job interviews? Don't say scientists didn't warn you about it. Wondering why you can't close a deal? Research says you need to close your mouth and listen!

Science is also showing us the power of impressions in the virtual world. In fact, the way you present yourself and your company online can be just as important as the real you. For example, we now have more data than ever on which online marketing strategies grow customers, engagement, satisfaction, and sales. We're also better at understanding the psychology behind why certain techniques, such as having authority figures validate your company, really work.

You might not be able to judge a book by its cover, but you can still determine whether it's a real book or just a couple of pieces of scrap paper held together with a rusty paper clip. In our fast-moving, information-overloaded world, customers don't have the bandwidth or the patience to look at what's between the covers. Successful entrepreneurs will have them at hello.

STRATEGIES TO MOBILIZE AND MOTIVATE YOUR CUSTOMERS

You may remember Starbucks' Unicorn Frappuccino. The limited-edition concoction, which changed colors and flavors with a simple stir, was a runaway success for the company—not only in terms of sales but also for the buzz it generated. Unicorn-crazed customers took to social media in droves, posting photos of the drink's many colorful variations. While the Unicorn Frappuccino was only on the market for less than a week in April 2017, its impact on consumers went far beyond that. Starbucks executive chairman Howard Schultz called the drink "the most stunning example of our understanding of digital and social media and Instagram."

The Unicorn Frappuccino wasn't an accident. Through research, analytics, and a little luck, Starbucks was able to tap into their customers' interests, encouraging them not only to buy the drink but to talk about it as well—the best marketing money can't buy.

How do you inspire your customers to not only evangelize for your brand on social media, but also to fill out surveys, join your mailing lists, write positive reviews, and tell their friends? In other words, how do you motivate them to work for you—for free? The answer lies in your ability to satisfy their needs and wants. Thankfully, research and analytics can make this process a little easier.

It all starts with understanding who your customers are and what they want. Thanks to the data collected online, you now have access to abundant information on your customers, such as their demographics, interests, likes, and dislikes. You can also identify and mobilize your influencers—those people who are active on social media and can promote your message and brand.

Research also gives entrepreneurs insight into the myriad ways your customers engage with your brand. Through methods such as frequent A/B testing and tweaking and improving your UX, you can learn what makes them tick and what makes them click. Look deep enough, and you will find research on practically every element of your consumers' behavior—from the colors and fonts that garner the best response to the messaging that most appeals to their emotions.

By understanding what motivates your customers and giving them what they want, you will begin to develop trust and loyalty. This is your holy grail. Satisfied customers will return again and again to your company and recommend you to their friends, family, and associates. And, as Starbucks proved, satisfied customers will post more than 180,000 outrageous photos of your product—all because they want to, not because you told them to.

RESEARCH FINDS SOCIAL MEDIA CAN MAKE YOU HAPPIER OR MISERABLE

Lesya Liu

Social media has many virtues and vices. Some believe people are becoming less social as a result of social media; others say it's bringing us closer than ever.

A study from the University of Leuven in Belgium found that Instagram can help adolescents cope with depression and social anxiety. In a large-scale study, youths were surveyed twice a year regarding their use of social media and their life contentment. Instagram usage correlated with feelings of friendship and closeness, which reduced depression.

In addition, a study out of the University of California, Berkeley's School of Information found that people actually feel more relaxed, more bored, and sleepier when they browse both Facebook and Twitter. Contrary to what you might read on your feed, these platforms actually made users wind down, not rev up.

Despite these encouraging results, the Belgian research team advised that if your Instagram usage doesn't make you feel closer to friends, it could actually be hurting you. A case in point: The most followed person on Instagram, singer Selena Gomez, who boasted 132 million followers as of 2018, told *Vogue* magazine in 2017 that the platform made her feel terrible about herself.

"It had become so consuming to me. It's what I woke up to and went to sleep to. I was an addict," she said. "I always end up feeling like shit when I look at Instagram. Which is why I'm kind of under the radar, ghosting it a bit."

So are we, as entrepreneurs, connecting with our customers on a new genuine level or are we chasing after likes? The answer is probably somewhere in between. Social media provides this unique instant gratification—as soon as you post something, people show you their support, approval, and admiration. This is especially true on Instagram, where a lot of individuals yearning to become Instafamous are participating in "follow-for-follow" schemes.

Because we want our business to look—and of course *be*—successful, we're after as many followers and likes as we can possibly get. It makes sense: People perceive "popular" things to be "great" and "cool." What we fail to recognize, though, is that we're going down a rabbit hole, always looking for more ways to be seen and liked by as many people as possible, whether or not it actually helps our business. This is, clearly, the wrong way to do social media.

The unmistakably correct way to do this social thing is to be sociable, to be of service, and to be authentic. Most Instafamous personalities and brands built their following on authenticity and connection. Maybe not all of them are connections we would care to make, but they know what audience they're after, and they know how to serve them each and every day to keep them coming back for more. "Follow-for-follow" schemes are a meaningless waste of time.

So if you want a large online following, home in on your audience and find what appeals to them. What do they find visually pleasing? What do they care about? What do they aspire to be? Soon enough your audience will feel that you "get" them, that you're one of theirs. This is how large followings are built.

If you are using Instagram—or any other social media platform, for that matter—to connect with people in your niche, it will show and will bring you closer to your audience. So don't forget that, as with anything in life, you need to strike a balance. Don't get obsessed over like and follower counts; spend your time creating and maintaining those human connections.

MOTIVATE CUSTOMERS TO BUY BASED ON THEIR BRAIN TYPE

Michael Cooper

Marketing your goods and services to specific brain types is a unique and powerful technique for communicating directly to what motivates people. If they aren't motivated to buy, odds are you won't sell much. Focusing on brain types is a great way to make sure your marketing speaks to people in a way that ultimately boosts sales.

Type 1: Controllers + Managers

This group wants to be in control and competitive with themselves and others. They want the best of everything. Status is important, so make sure to communicate how your products or services will help them reach their goals, gain prestige, or save time and money. They will often share their experience, but only to close, trusted friends and colleagues. Use language that communicates achievement, luxury, and status.

Type 2: Innovators + Influencers

Unique experiences and whatever is new and interesting draw people with this brain type. They are early adopters and like being on the cutting edge. Communicate how your products or services are different and exclusive, or provide an interesting and distinctive experience that they can share with others.

Innovators + Influencers naturally connect with a wide range of people and are comfortable influencing others to purchase goods or services, so be sure to make it easy for them to spread the word about your wares: social-media profiles, refer-a-friend links, and ways to add their own experiences to your website or product listings.

Type 3: Nurturers + Harmonizers

This group tends to buy and adopt products that are reliable and proven. When marketing to this type, play up close relationships and being included, and be sure to provide lots of testimonials from other people like them. Demonstrate how your goods and services will make their lives easier, cultivate great relationships, build community, and help others. They often don't make purchasing decisions on their own—relying heavily on the suggestions of others and online reviews before deciding to buy. Make sure this information is easy to find so that they are comfortable buying from you.

Type 4: Systemizers + Analyzers

People with this brain type avoid risks and rarely try unproven products or services. They dislike being wrong, so offer money-back guarantees and trials of products and services if possible. They need proof, including case studies, testimonials, and technical documentation that what you're offering is reliable and safe. They are also very cost conscious and will even use a spreadsheet to compare features and prices on similar products—be sure to provide as much information as possible so they can consider your products or services carefully.

Systemizers + Analyzers are typically very thorough when investigating a product; they take time to make a decision, often visiting websites several times and reading all your product data and online reviews. Make sure this information is easily accessible to better market to this type.

Unless you sell a commodity product or service, it's rare that your core customers will span across several brain types. However, if they do, you must weave their needs together to communicate your value. The bottom line: If your customers can't see how a product is valuable to them, they won't buy it.

ANALYZING THE SCIENCE BEHIND CUSTOMER LOYALTY

Chris Poelma

Raise your hand if you've built up an extensive collection of loyalty punch cards through the years. I know I'm guilty. From free T-shirts to free meals, getting something complimentary from a business you frequent is always awesome. The trouble is that I—like everyone else—get busy and forget about those punch cards I've squirreled away; I even sometimes forget about the business that provided them in the first place. The moral of the story: If you're trying to figure out a strategy to better harvest customer loyalty, this isn't the best tactic.

As a business owner, the most reliable tool in your arsenal for attracting, engaging, and retaining customers is the data you aggregate about them. In fact, a study from *Forbes* reported that organizations that are taking a data-driven approach have higher levels of customer engagement and market growth than their old-school competitors.

Today's consumer is a whole new breed. With the advent of advanced, real-time technology, consumers have come to expect a more personalized experience from the businesses they buy from—especially those they turn to most often. This might seem like a tall order—particularly for smaller businesses that are just starting out—but when used correctly, incorporating data into your relationships with customers can spur increased loyalty. Here are a few tips to make analytics your ally in retaining multidimensional customers.

Start Small

Think your business is too small to get overwhelmed by customer-related data? Think again. From in-store and online transactions to inventory, marketing, and overall service performance, there is a lot for business owners to analyze when it comes to how well they're resonating with customers. While all the information you aggregate is important to some degree, you'll have better success—and save your sanity—by prioritizing the right type of data and moving the needle on just a few key customer-driven metrics.

For me, service and product satisfaction have always been the most critical components to measure throughout the lifetime of a business. Over the years, I've deployed a variety of tactics to gather customer sentiment, but the most tried-and-true method has been surveys. They serve as a catchall for understanding your customers' likes, dislikes, and general personas. While there is always a debate regarding what question provides the most insight into customer satisfaction, I take my cue from Fred Reichheld, author of *The Ultimate Question*, and analyze responses regarding how likely my customers are to recommend my business to others.

Advancements in customer-facing technology, like point-of-sale (POS) solutions or online shopping carts, make it easy and less cumbersome to capture customer satisfaction information, among other data, following the point of purchase.

Predict and Prescribe Success

More and more technology platforms are putting analytics at the forefront and making it easier for business users to access and make data more actionable—which is huge for businesses with limited resources.

The perfect solution can provide both predictive and prescriptive analytics on your customers based on historical data. Both types of analytics serve a purpose when it comes to fostering the loyalty of your customers. Predictive analytics forecasts what action a customer will take based on past behavioral data. You can use this intel to analyze customer order histories, for example, gaining a better understanding of trending peak times of purchase and products purchased, in order to make more strategic buying decisions.

Prescriptive analytics takes things a step further, providing recommended actions for you (or your customer) based on past behavioral and predictive data. Think about Amazon's "Recommendations for You" or Facebook's "People You May Know." Those are prescriptive analytics at work. This type of insight helps you deliver the personalized experience your customers crave and provides you with a competitive advantage.

Find Your Customers to Round Out Your Omnichannel Approach

Using analytics to determine where customers are interacting with your brand can also set your business apart and drive loyalty in the eyes of today's multidimensional consumer. For example, reviewing things like survey responses to determine how a customer prefers to be reached, or analyzing the number of purchases and/or support requests made through a specific channel like mobile compared to other methods will paint a good picture of how best to communicate with your customers.

This information builds the framework for a successful omnichannel strategy, which you'll need to keep customers coming back. According to an Aberdeen Group study, companies with extremely strong omnichannel customer engagement retain on average 89 percent of their customers, compared to 33 percent for companies with weak omnichannel customer engagement.

We took this approach at our company when determining the best channels to provide customer support. After some research and data analysis, we realized the majority of our customers would prefer to text their support requests as opposed to calling a support line or sending an email. With that in mind, we added text to chat capabilities to our existing live call center and online chat functionality.

Face the Facts

Ultimately, when you focus on gathering the right data, making the information actionable, and using it to develop an omnichannel strategy, the true understanding your business has for its customers will shine through. It's time to recycle those lame old punch cards and divert your attention to a more practical means for engaging existing loyal customers and generating new ones.

23

PERSUADING CUSTOMERS TO TELL YOUR STORY IS BECOMING A SCIENCE

Dan Blacharski

Years ago, before there were such things as social media, user reviews, and the internet, there was a men's store in my hometown of South Bend, Indiana. Their tagline was "one man tells another." They were ahead of their time: That simple phrase is at the very heart of today's socially driven marketing.

What that store knew then and what companies are today beginning to acknowledge is that the best advertisement for your brand isn't going to come from TV, print, or banner ads. The best advertisement is when one man (or woman) tells another about your business.

Relying on customers instead of an ad agency to spread the word is risky business, since you lose an element of control over the conversation. But consumers give more weight to a personal recommendation than a TV commercial, and because of the prevalence of online user reviews and review platforms like CrowdReviews.com, which take extra steps to ensure a review's legitimacy, buying decisions are heavily influenced by this type of social user-generated content.

What's Wrong with TV Ads?

There's a logic behind the move toward direct social engagement tactics like user reviews, and it's because younger demographics just don't respond to TV commercials. A Boston Consulting Group survey showed that Millennials engage with brands more deeply than do Baby Boomers. Fifty-two percent of Millennials use social media on their mobile devices to note that they like a brand, while only 33 percent of Boomers do so; 39 percent of Millennials post product reviews. According to the BCG report,

"It is more difficult through traditional marketing to convince a U.S. Millennial than an older U.S. consumer that a brand is relevant to him or her. Millennials turn to much wider networks for advice."

Historically, a common tactic in advertising was to provide testimonials from experts, which, for a time, was successful. In a 1949 TV commercial, for example, consumers were told that doctors prefer Camel cigarettes over other tobacco brands; that approach would never work on Millennials today. "Millennials care less about what the experts say and more about what their peers say," says Carlos Garay, CEO of SOURCEvapes, one of the biggest brands of vaping products; his company uses product reviews as part of its marketing strategy.

"The key to a review strategy is maintaining the integrity of the reviews," Garay says. "Our strategy is simple. We just ask consumers to write a review after a purchase, and we've found that in most cases, they are willing to do so. We have over 5,600 verified reviews, the most of any vaporizer company, with a five-star average. This kind of customer validation and attention to quality has made us the number-one brand for enthusiasts of hemp-derived CBD wax."

SOURCEvapes' basic tactic is simple, straight-forward, and nonintrusive. A simple auto-emailing system sends a short, friendly note, asking customers to leave a review. SOURCEvapes has partnered with Yotpo, a consumer-content marketing platform, which also increases the credibility of the reviews by showing reviews from verified buyers—and it simplifies the process by providing customers with an easy link to click on if they want to leave a review.

What Review Sites Do You Want to Be On?

Larger review sites like CrowdReviews.com, Yelp!, or Angie's List are some of the best-known brands, and directing users to one of those gives you a better chance of recognition and the benefit of association with a well-known brand, as well as added credibility due to their vetting process. In the case of CrowdReviews, the site verifies reviewers' identities as well as the legitimacy of the companies being reviewed.

While those larger sites typically offer reviews in multiple product or service categories, smaller sites may cater to a specific niche, specializing in reviewing everything from tobacco vaping products to mattresses. In addition to appearing on the broader review sites, marketers may also wish to incorporate select niche review sites into the mix. I spoke with the webmaster of niche review site Best Mattress Brand, who offered some insight into how marketers are using these types of sites to help create brand awareness. Since most of these smaller sites are not as well known, he says it is important for the marketer to choose a review site that offers in-depth information, well-written and detailed reviews and articles, and an unbiased look at companies and products.

Finally, there are spam review sites that should be avoided at all costs. These are the ones with thinly written reviews (many of which are obviously fake) and what are clearly paid affiliate links to each company's website. Affiliate relationships are not an indication that a review site isn't credible, but if there is a relationship, it should be plainly disclosed.

User Review Best Practices

Consider these strategies if you want your customers to leave more reviews:

First, encourage the social conversation and become a part of it, but don't try to control it. Trying to force direction, editing or deleting posts, or paying for positive reviews are all tactics that run contrary to the sentiment of social advertising and user-generated content.

Gently encourage your customers' participation. Ask for the review without being demanding or needy.

Make it easy for them to participate. Use tools like Yotpo to auto-email customers after a purchase, and give them a quick link so they can submit a review easily.

Never buy reviews or offer incentives. If word gets out that you're buying fake reviews (which tend to be pretty transparent and obvious), or even that you are giving incentives or free products in exchange for positive reviews, you will instantly lose all credibility. The reviews must be organic for them to have any meaning.

Finally, carefully select the review sites you want to direct customers to. Review sites should have transparent policies on how they determine rankings and what their financial relationships are with brands.

Happy customers who speak highly of your brand are the best advertising money can't buy. People will always trust a friend's recommendation more than an anonymous advertiser. If you can encourage your customers to evangelize for you for free, you will have saved yourself a ton of money.

THE SCIENCE BEHIND HIGH-CONVERTING WEBSITES

Eric Samson

If you're a business owner with a world-class product, a solid marketing strategy, and the perfect price point to make the product both attractive and profitable, you may well be wondering, "What's next?" But if yours is a web-based business, "what's next" has to be what you can do to enable customers to purchase your offerings as easily as possible.

And unfortunately for both consumers and business owners, many websites just aren't built to emphasize such conversions. Instead, they're hampered by everything from shoddy design to glitchy shopping carts. And that's a serious problem, because a poorly built website can be the downfall of a company—like yours—that has everything else going for it.

Done right, on the other hand, conversion-rate optimization can be seamless and provide value both to the customer (in the form of convenience and speed) and the company (revenue).

Here are a few of the key components found in high-converting websites.

Clickworthy Calls to Action

It is estimated that Amazon's "Buy now with 1-click" button has generated billions of dollars of additional revenue for the company over the years, and part of the reason it works so well is that it sends a strong signal to customers just when they are ready to purchase.

This is the meaning of a "call to action" (CTA). But it's important to know that CTAs don't always have to come at the moment of purchase. You can also encourage newsletter subscriptions, for instance, with a prominently placed pop-up.

Consumer-Friendly Colors

Color plays a significant role in human psychology, and up to 85 percent of consumers list color as a top reason for purchasing a product. High-converting websites contain detailed product photos with colors that pop and also effectively use color in the design of the website to encourage buying behavior.

Email Lead Capture and Remarketing

Well-timed email marketing campaigns lead to healthy conversion rates, so make sure your email messaging is precisely targeted to your audience. Many successful product-based companies also send out automated emails in the event of an abandoned shopping cart, typically offering an additional discount if the customer returns to purchase within a certain time frame.

Frequent Testing

Every aspect of the browsing and purchasing experience needs to be thoroughly tested multiple times prior to the website's implementation. It's always helpful to get feedback from unbiased users, who will generally be more than willing to tell you if anything would stop them from making a purchase.

Mobile-Friendly Navigation and Shopping

As a new generation of consumers raised on mobile devices gains purchasing power, mobile commerce is becoming increasingly important. Not only do mobile devices now account for approximately 33 percent of all online sales, but nearly half of all traffic on websites is now generated from a phone or tablet.

If your customers are unable to purchase your product from their phones just as easily as from their laptops, they will inevitably look for other options.

Post-Purchase Service

Your relationship with customers doesn't end after they go through checkout. You can use the post-purchase landing page to foster customer loyalty and encourage repeat purchases. This space can be used to once again encourage email sign-up, if customers haven't completed it already.

Furthermore, you can share links directing visitors to customer service or product-related information to help them better understand how to use and take care of their purchase.

Reliable Shopping Carts

Many retailers make the mistake of thinking they are home free once a customer adds an item to an online cart, but shopping cart abandonment is rife throughout the digital commerce industry. Some experts estimate that more than 60 percent of the more than $4 trillion left in shopping carts in one year could be turned into sales with the proper tactics.

One effective technique is to do everything possible to have shoppers create an account with your business, so their information can be saved for easy checkout in the future.

Secure Checkout

As incidents involving data breaches by hackers litter the evening news, technophiles and technophobes alike have become more concerned about the security of their data, especially that tied to credit cards and other financial information.

Make an investment in secure checkout procedures and prominently place the logos of your security partners on the page to assure customers that you take the protection of their personal information seriously.

Targeted Landing Pages

Once you have done the hard work of getting your customers to click on your ad or promotional email, make sure it sends them to a page that will facilitate their purchase. It sounds simple enough, but you'd be surprised how many companies make customers navigate from the homepage after sending them an email with a special product promotion.

It may not seem like much time for a customer to spend in the grand scheme of things, but there is no reason to put an obstacle in their way once they have made the decision to check out your latest offerings.

Usable Interface

In a broad sense, a successful website should be responsive, easy to navigate, and free of any clutter that could confuse the shopper. A new customer should be able to come to your website for the first time, intuitively navigate through various sections, and place something in a shopping cart in a matter of seconds. Above all, she should never have to search the page to figure out how to purchase a product.

As you can see, a lot can go wrong between the customer's decision to buy your product and the actual purchase. It's easy to get so bogged down with making sure your product is attractive that you put less focus on the geeky stuff like UX, UI, and conversion optimization. But if your customers are bouncing from your site at a high rate and leaving their shopping carts full, you'd be well-served to invest more time and energy into making sure the purchasing experience is as seamless and easy as possible.

FIVE WAYS TO MAXIMIZE WORD-OF-MOUTH MARKETING

Brian Sutter

For as long as any of us can remember, we've been relying on recommendations from family and friends for everything from cars to toothpaste. At one time, this type of word-of-mouth review was simple and straightforward. Then technology entered the picture, the way we interact with one another changed drastically, and it became easier to discount the human aspect of marketing and business.

In our tech-driven world, people are more widely connected than ever. It's not just about creating messages—it's about delivering real human experiences to the masses. Smart marketers and business owners who can figure this out are the ones using the most influential form of information consumers rely on when making purchase decisions: word-of-mouth marketing.

If that sounds simple, don't be fooled—it isn't. Creating cutting-edge buzz-worthy messages that go viral is no easy task.

According to a 2018 article from *Small Business Trends*, Sageworks banking software reports indicate that the average small business dedicates a mere 1 percent of revenue to advertising and marketing. When they do invest, most of these business owners are likely thinking about traditional forms of advertising or collecting new customers instead of connecting with them.

How do you turn consumers into passionate brand advocates through word-of-mouth marketing? How do you fuel conversations that make people want to share your message with their network? Consider how the five thoughtful word-of-mouth campaigns below connected with consumers on a human level and, in turn, generated massive awareness and profits for their brands.

1. Identify and Target Your Influencers

An influencer is someone who is active on social media and blogs and is able to promote your message and brand. Marketing expert Jay Baer probably put it best when he said, "True influence drives action, not just awareness." The truth is, consumers today trust a third party much more than they trust brands. Getting the right message out to influencers is a new way of marketing that, if done effectively, can lead to explosive growth for businesses.

Take for example Reckitt Benckiser's brand Dettol. The company found that its liquid antiseptic was struggling to grow in China outside the most populous cities. Furthermore, its extremely pricey TV ads weren't building the kind of brand awareness Reckitt Benckiser needed. Reckitt Benckiser eventually teamed up with marketing firm Advocacy WOM to plan a word-of-mouth campaign focused on influencer moms.

The company distributed 48,000 samples to 4,000 influencer moms, who each received one kit for herself and ten more for her friends. The campaign was a massive success, reaching 46 percent of the brand's target audience. In five months, brand awareness increased five times, purchases doubled from 21 percent to 42 percent, and sales increased 86 percent in only two months.

2. Connect to the Human Emotion

The Make-A-Wish Foundation is well-known for its dedication to granting wishes to children facing life-threatening illnesses. Making people aware of your brand is one thing—staying in the conversation is another. To achieve the latter, the nonprofit organization created a compelling event for Miles Scott, a five-year-old cancer survivor in remission, who wished he could be the superhero Batkid for one day.

On November 15, 2013, Make-A-Wish created one of its largest events ever, turning San Francisco into Gotham City for a day. It included participation from then-President Barack Obama and other government officials and law enforcement. Even the city's main newspaper, the *San Francisco Chronicle*, produced a "Gotham City Chronicle" edition with the headline "Batkid Saves City: Hooded hero nabs Riddler, rescues damsel in distress."

As a result of its extraordinary word-of-mouth campaign, Make-A-Wish received 1.89 million social impressions, 555,697 #batkid hashtags, significant press coverage including a BuzzFeed article that generated 2.5 million hits within three days, more than 21,683 Instagram and Twitter photos posted by the end of the day—and, of course, increased donations.

3. Continuously Involve Communities

People never stop talking about Red Bull because the energy drink company, Red Bull GmbH, literally never stops hosting festive events that get people involved. Among some of the initiatives that keep Red Bull as the industry's market leader are:

- A *Red Bull Wings Team* that drives around Red Bull branded vehicles distributing samples while having fun and generating buzz
- A *Red Bull Student Brand Manager* program that sponsors students to build awareness at events near their campus
- A *Red Bull Bedroom Jam*, which hosts talent show events that target students
- A *Red Bull Reporter program*, which sponsors journalism and film students to create stories and buzz for the brand

Another example of a word-of-mouth campaign that involved communities effectively is when Vail Resorts created an online and mobile app that connected skiers with their networks on the mountain. In 2010, Vail launched EpicMix, which used RFID technology embedded into season passes and lift tickets to allow riders to learn where and when they rode and how far they traveled, which motivated and challenged riders to push themselves while sharing their stories and achievements with their friends and family.

After going live in December 2010, 100,000 guests—or 15 percent of total eligible guests—activated accounts on EpicMix and generated more than 35 million social impressions.

4. Give Consumers Something to Talk About with Superior Customer Service

A 2015 report found that the probability you'll sell to an existing customer is 60 to 70 percent, while that number falls to between 5 and 20 percent for new customers.

Based on these numbers, businesses should be focused on creating customer service that transforms customers into fans who can't stop talking about your brand. It's not so much about gifts and promotions, but how you communicate and treat the people who keep your business afloat.

5. Make It Easy for People to Leave Reviews

One of the worst things you can do in a word-of-mouth campaign is make it difficult for consumers to leave reviews and recommendations and communicate with one another about your brand. Simplify the process for customers to interact with brands, much in the way 3M ESPE, a manufacturer of dental products, did when it tweaked its online review process to only require an email address. They made the process so simple that the company increased customer review volume on its products by 200 percent in three days.

Word-of-mouth is the oldest form of advertising, and it's still instrumental to getting your message out there in today's technological, fast-paced world. The difference is, how do you get people to care when you're not giving them the message face-to-face? The above examples are excellent go-to case studies of successful word-of-mouth marketing campaigns.

When all else fails, think about what people are talking about. What's in the news? What are people sharing on social media? Consider coming up with a campaign to piggyback off of conversations that are already happening, as Starbucks did when it announced its baristas are encouraged to talk about race with customers. Whether this was a good or bad move for the coffee giant, it generated massive media coverage and got the public talking.

No matter how advanced our technology becomes, it's important for brands to understand that they're still connecting with humans. In other words, forget about the followers and "likes" everyone else is trying to gain, and focus on deeper insight—think about what people want to talk about and identify the people who can help you get your message out there.

FIVE SIMPLE TIPS YOU CAN USE TO CAPTURE THE ATTENTION OF MILLENNIALS

Jonathan Long

There is nonstop chatter these days about how Millennials are a completely different breed of consumer, but that conversation often ends without an explanation of how to get on their radar. It's well worth your time and effort to connect with Millennials, though—they are America's largest generation.

There are several simple rules that can help your business connect with Millennials—here are five that can be implemented by any business.

1. Support a Social Cause

Millennials are huge supporters of brands that try to make a positive impact—both nationally and at a local community level. Something as simple as donating a small percentage of proceeds to a good cause can do wonders when it comes to Millennial acceptance. If you support a cause, they will, in turn, support your business.

Christopher VanDeCar, CEO of Optimally Organic, has seen this trend increase. "It goes beyond just monetary donations. Simply showing support for a cause can also help attract the attention of Millennials," says VanDeCar. "Millennials connect with brands that share their same values. They are a very socially aware generation."

2. Adopt a Mobile-First Marketing Strategy

Most internet searches begin on a mobile device these days, and nobody is more connected to mobile phones than Millennials. This isn't going to change— in fact, it's only going to be an increasing trend. If you want to be successful in the digital world, you must implement a mobile-first marketing strategy.

You need to design everything, from your website's look to your offers, with mobile users in mind. If you don't, your user experience will be poor and you will see the Millennial generation quickly disconnect from your brand. New startups understand this, but older brands need to quickly convert to this way of thinking or risk completely alienating themselves from the Millennial consumer market.

3. Be Very Active on Social Media

Social media is part of every Millennial's life. They are extremely active on Facebook, Twitter, Instagram, Snapchat, and Pinterest. They spend hours on social media every single day, making it crucial that you are there as well. You must have an active social media marketing plan that is designed to attract, engage, and convert Millennials.

Not only can you use social media to place your brand in front of Millennials, but you can also use it to create content that triggers engagement—Millennials love to share, and if your message resonates with them, it can lead to free exposure.

4. Create Visual Content

Content marketing is good for your business, but rather than focusing solely on blog posts, shift your focus to creating visual content. One study revealed that content containing images receives 94 percent more views than content without. This includes video, graphics, and pictures.

Video content is becoming increasingly popular, and infographics are still some of the most-shared pieces of content on most blogs. Creating video content can also help you establish a personal connection. Giving your audience a look at the behind-the-scenes, day-to-day operation of your business makes you appear more human, which is something that really appeals to Millennials. You don't need a huge budget—many brands are crushing it by creating content from mobile devices and editing and uploading it with free apps.

5. Let Your Data Dictate Your Direction

There is a sea of data available right at your fingertips. Sadly, most businesses don't even look at it, let alone take advantage of it. Most social media networks have analytics available to you as a business owner—knowing what posts receive the most engagement and what content is shared most often can help you stay on track and publish future content that your audience enjoys.

You can add Google Analytics to your email campaign manager to view data and gain insights to evaluate performance and map out future efforts. For example, if you are noticing a high bounce rate on a web page from traffic coming from a Facebook post, you know that there is a disconnect somewhere and you will need to make a change.

SEVEN SCIENCE-BACKED STRATEGIES FOR DEALING WITH ANGRY CUSTOMERS

Tobi Abdulgafar

The goal of the average freelancer, entrepreneur, or service provider can be summed up in this basic algorithm: Get a client, land a gig, get the job done, get paid promptly, and get a repeat.

If you hope to achieve that goal, the last thing you want to do is incur your client's wrath. There's a problem, though: Some clients can always find a reason to blow a fuse. It doesn't matter if you're the greatest freelancer in your niche or have more than a decade of experience. You could have Albert Einstein's intellect and Leonardo da Vinci's creativity combined, delivering impeccable services well before deadline. And there still might be one or two clients you simply can't please.

Not to worry. Science assures us these seven methods can help defuse your customer's rage and calm your own frustration levels, too.

1. Calm the Heck Down

Suppose an angry client calls and starts yelling about how dissatisfied he is with your service and quality of work. Most people's automatic reaction is to yell back. Don't. Don't say a word, and don't interrupt. Let your customer vent. Research shows that your ability to think critically and make intelligent decisions plummets when you let anger drive your actions.

These conversations can snowball into shouting contests that leave both of you bitter and the issue unreconciled. They can also rule out any possibility of repeat business in the future.

2. Listen

Now that you're calm, make a conscious attempt to listen to your client as she enumerates everything that went wrong. Active listening is a proven way to influence your clients and win them over. It goes well beyond keeping quiet and giving someone your full attention. It requires stamina, patience, and concentration. FBI negotiators use active listening to de-escalate hostage situations and save lives.

It might help to grab a writing pad and jot down a few notes as you listen. This ensures you won't forget any important details as you think about possible solutions to the problem. Freelancers who embrace the high art of listening usually have a healthier annual bottom line.

3. Ask Questions

Rather than make defensive statements that try to shift the blame away from yourself, ask open-ended questions: "What would you like me to do?" or "How would you like me to remedy the situation?" are good places to start. This will loosen up your client because it creates a strong impression you're on their side. Once you learn how they would like the error to be corrected, offer some extra help at your expense. Thank them for the feedback and offer a genuine apology for the mishap.

4. Try Some (Internal) Humor

According to the American Psychological Association, humor can help reduce tension in high-pressure situations. It can also help restore a more balanced perspective. If you find yourself thinking of a customer as a single-celled life form, try to imagine what that would actually look like. Picture an amoeba sitting at a desk and talking on the phone—even doodle a sketch. Doing so might take the edge off your fury and make you open to a discussion that leads to a mutually agreeable resolution.

We've all heard laughter is the best medicine. It relieves stress, elevates mood, enhances creativity, and makes you more resilient. Just take care not to use harsh or sarcastic humor with your customers. That's another form of aggression, and your client might interpret your attempt to be clever as dismissive.

5. Don't Take It Personally

Realize that your customer isn't trying to assassinate your character. The anger she is feeling has little to do with you on a personal level, so don't beat yourself up. Sure, your client feels bad about services you or your staff performed. But is the problem necessarily with you as an individual? No.

In fact, there are times another person's rage isn't about you at all. Recognizing this can have a major influence on your coping abilities. A 2012 study revealed that people who understood they didn't cause another person's anger weren't upset by the situation.

6. Know When to Disengage

"In any exchange with an overly angry person, there may come a point when you need to disengage from the situation," says professor and anger researcher Ryan Martin. As chair of the psychology program at the University of Wisconsin-Green Bay, he studies many different facets of the anger experience, including the consequences of problematic anger and how people express their anger online.

There are several reasons that disengaging might be the smartest move. First, you need to stay safe and protect yourself. Second, the chance of a positive outcome decreases the longer the situation goes on. Your client may be so angry that a healthy, reasonable conversation simply isn't possible in the moment. If that's the case, it's best to suggest, "Let's talk about this later when we're both calmer." Then move on.

7. Let Your Client Have the Last Word

Wrap up the conversation on a good note by allowing your client to have the last word. If you absolutely must offer a final comment, take care not to make it a defensive statement. He is likely to see through you if you use your last words to summarize why you're right and he is wrong. Clinical psychologist Albert J. Bernstein says this is a good way to send your client back into "attack mode" and scuttle all the progress you've made. His book *Dinosaur Brains: Dealing with All Those Impossible People at Work* explains the brain science behind confrontations and suggests productive ways to handle difficult discussions in the workplace.

It can be hard to be berated by a customer, especially when they're rude and wrong. But learning how to effectively defuse an angry client will help to calm them down and teach you how to manage your own emotions.

THE SCIENCE BEHIND CUSTOMER CHURN

Luc Burgelman

Every successful business puts the customers first, which means today's consumers are unequivocally in the driver's seat. With fewer and fewer incentives to stay loyal, all it takes is one less-than-positive interaction and your customer can easily move on. The reality is that it costs significantly more money to acquire new customers than retain existing ones, and it costs far more to reacquire customers who have defected.

That's why you need to start focusing on reducing customer churn, if you haven't already.

The Key Issue: Knowing Your Customer

In order to identify early signs of potential churn, you first need to start getting a holistic view of your customers and their interactions across multiple channels, such as store/branch visits, product purchase history, calls to customer service, web-based transactions, and social media interactions, to name a few. Let's take a look at the banking industry, for example.

The ability to track customer sentiment gives banks early indicators into customer service issues and/or opportunities for greater engagement. It allows them to be proactive in improving the customer experience and to continuously monitor engagement with the brand, which can highlight potential indicators of customer churn, such as:

- Recent dramatic decrease in the assets in a customer's accounts
- Cancellation of automatic incoming credits or outgoing payments
- Negative interactions on customer calls
- Drop-off in web-based banking activities
- Drop-off in mobile payments and the value of mobile transactions

However, the information about a customer's sentiment and their experience across multiple channels lies in many structured and unstructured data sources. The information could be in the form of logs from a customer's bank visits, call center and website interactions, tweets, Facebook interactions, community forums, customer emails, and customer surveys. Disparate and fast-moving data stored in silos makes it challenging for banks to get a holistic understanding of their customers, understand the shift in sentiment, or detect early warning signs and proactively engage them with retention or cross-sell marketing offers.

How Big Data Can Help You Predict Potential Churn

The sheer volume of customer data available to companies has made it almost impossible to store, analyze, and retrieve meaningful insights using traditional data management technologies. But now, big data can help you solve these challenges, allowing you to leverage both structured and unstructured data from multiple channels.

Native big data technologies solve the data management challenges by storing, analyzing, and retrieving the massive volume and variety of structured and unstructured data, scaling elastically as the data grows. Additionally, sophisticated data-matching capabilities allow you to eliminate the data silos, connect the dots of a customer's interactions across multiple channels, and build a comprehensive holistic customer profile.

Now What?

The question remains—is this holistic view enough to predict potential churners in an efficient manner? It all comes down to changing the way we work. Introducing newer technologies can help us, but it won't do much if we stick to traditional ways of thinking. It's only doing more of the same—with more data and more people.

Traditional approaches meant building models to identify high-risk churn targets. But very often you discovered them after the damage was already done. Today you must go beyond accumulating insights and apply your customer analytics to your process. That means in real time, on an individual level, and in the process of your customer interaction. Doing so will help you pinpoint exactly where and why they turn and what their next move is; you can then target them with relevant messages or offers at exactly the right time to prevent churn.

Ultimately, customer intelligence management and the use of real-time big data and machine learning give companies a distinct competitive advantage with the ability to prevent churn, drive cross selling, and build customer loyalty. After all, smart businesses know that the first purchase is really just the beginning; the real business value lies in retaining that customer.

ENTREPRENEUR VOICES SPOTLIGHT: INTERVIEW WITH PAUL SCHEMPP

Director of Sport Instruction Research Lab at the University of Georgia

Paul G. Schempp, Ph.D., is an expert in expertise. As director of the Sport Instruction Research Laboratory at the University of Georgia and author of six books, including *5 Steps to Expert: How to Go from Business Novice to Elite Performer*, he's spent more than a decade researching the characteristics and skills of successful people in the business, sports, and education arenas. "We really try to focus on how successful people learn and develop," he says.

As an academic and inspirational speaker, he's studied and met with many successful, and not so successful, people over the years. Here are some of his most interesting findings.

Entrepreneur: How important is knowledge to success?

Schempp: One of the key characteristics for people of success is that they are consummate learners. We asked elite coaches in both tennis and golf how they ranked, on a scale of 1 to 10, in terms of knowledge—10 being that they knew everything there was to know about the sport and how to coach it; 1 being that they knew almost nothing. Then we asked the same question to novices who had been coaching one year or less. The surprising finding was that the experts ranked themselves an average of 4.5, while the novices ranked themselves at 8.5. Successful people are always trying to learn more. The danger in the novices' answer is that when you think you know all there is to know, how hard do you try to learn more?

Entrepreneur: You've found that good decision making is a key component to success. Talk to us about that.

Schempp: The ability to make a decision is a skill—you're not born with it, you learn how to do it. Highly successful people are very good at eliminating distraction. They focus on solving the problem long term. Studies at the University of Pittsburgh found that people who are highly successful spend more time defining the problem. They don't guess. They want to make sure they have the problem right, because if they don't have the problem right, there's no hope of getting the solution right.

Highly successful people are able to identify the factors that are causing the problem, because that leads them to understanding what they need to do to eliminate this problem and make the changes that will make them successful. When they come up with potential solutions, they usually don't go with the first decision they think of. They deliberate on it. People who are less successful at decision making only make one decision. They leave themselves no other options, and usually drive that one decision into the ground.

Entrepreneur: You're also a big proponent of finding mentors.

Schempp: One of the things we discovered in highly successful people is that they all gave a lot of credit to their mentors. They felt they could not have learned the skills, knowledge values, and standards and navigated their successful career without some level of mentoring to guide them. We did a study with NFL coaches and found that the most successful coaches had between three and five mentors. One or two wasn't enough. It gave them restricted perspective. And if they had more than five mentors, it was too many voices in the choir.

These coaches had mentors for different things, not just football. It's important to be mentored by people outside your field. For example, if I wanted to start a chain of pizza stores, I might look for someone similar who started a chain of sunglasses stores. Why? Someone inside your field may be a competitor and less likely to want to share their secrets.

Entrepreneur: Are there any qualities of successful people that you know to be true anecdotally, but you can't measure?

Schempp: Passion. Successful people have a deep passion for what they do that transcends more than what you might call the "external factors of success." They don't do it so that their bank account is big, or so that people think they're wonderful; they do it because they truly love what they do.

PART III
STRATEGIES TO MOBILIZE AND MOTIVATE YOUR CUSTOMERS— REFLECTIONS

Science can help entrepreneurs achieve customer growth, customer loyalty, and customer action. You literally can't afford to ignore it. According to one study, organizations that are data-driven report much higher levels of customer engagement and market growth than their "laggard" competitors. The most valuable secret weapon in your stockpile is the information you've collected about your consumers: what they like, what they want, and what they need. By understanding what motivates the decisions and choices they make, you understand how to satisfy their needs.

The research is everywhere, but you have to know what to look for and what to do with the information. For example, we know now that there is a science behind websites with high conversion rates. Studies have looked at the effectiveness of certain colors, fonts, designs, and messaging to influence behavior.

Science also tells us the importance of making a personal connection with customers. Today's consumers don't want to feel sold to; they want to feel like they're part of a community or a cause. Companies like Red Bull host events all over the world to entertain, engage with, and interact with their consumers.

A happy customer is a loyal customer. And a loyal customer will do much more than buy your product. They will spread the word and become a brand ambassador. They'll tell your story for you in the form of positive reviews, flattering tweets and Instagram posts, and good old-fashioned word-of-mouth.

MINDSETS THAT CREATE BALANCE

The 40-hour workweek is so . . . 1940. That was the year the U.S. Congress amended the Fair Labor Standards Act to limit the workweek to 40 hours. My, how things have changed. Back here in the 21st century, a Harvard Business School survey of 1,000 professionals found that 94 percent worked at least 50 hours a week, and almost half worked more than 65 hours. To most entrepreneurs trying to get ahead, those numbers probably sound like a holiday.

One of the great American values is rolling up your sleeves and getting the job done. Thomas Edison was believed to have said, "There is no substitute for hard work." While it's true there can't be success without sweat, new science also shows us that all work and no play can actually be counterproductive and ruinous to our health. Thought leaders across the business spectrum are emphasizing the importance of work-life balance. They point to research challenging our assumptions about the relationship between success and time spent working. And they are redefining what it means to be "successful" in the first place.

Intuitively, most of us know that success is more than just scaling our business and watching the money flow into our bank account. Science is now proving this as well. Studies show that being optimistic, feeling self-confident, and having the freedom to do things you enjoy correlate directly with success. Thriving entrepreneurs know when to hit the pause button. They have other interests besides the bottom line. They enjoy learning and mastering new skills or simply unplugging and enjoying the moment.

It isn't easy to find this balance. In these days of smartphones and wifi, the business day never stops, and we're expected to be on all the time. How do you leave work at work when work is always in your pocket? We also live in a culture that doesn't emphasize having a life outside of work. Case in point: When you meet someone at a party, what's usually the first question they ask? "So, what do you do?" And they're not referring to your hobbies or your fitness regimen. We are all so hyperfocused on our jobs and our work that it's become commonplace to describe ourselves as "swamped"—not as a bad thing, but as a badge of honor.

Thankfully, this paradigm is starting to shift. The same technology that has made us beholden to work is also helping free us from its grip. Forward-thinking companies are implementing policies that encourage interests and activities beyond the cubicle. Researchers are discovering the benefits of taking short breaks, vacations, and even naps. While we may never return to the 40-hour workweek of 1940, we seem to be entering a new era where taking care of yourself is as important as taking care of business.

In the following chapters, our writers offer suggestions for bringing balance back into the seesaw of your life. And if you're concerned that this might be a bunch of mumbo-jumbo about getting spa treatments and going for nature hikes, keep reading. We think you'll like what you learn.

29

STRESSED OUT? SCIENCE SAYS TO PLAY A VIDEO GAME FOR FIVE MINUTES

Stephen J. Bronner

It's great when science gives credence to the things you already do. The latest example of this in my own life comes in the form of a study backing up what I and other scientists already know: Playing video games helps you relax.

Research led by Michael Rupp, a doctoral student in human factors and cognitive psychology at the University of Central Florida, and published in *Human Factors*, found that study participants who took a break from mentally taxing work and played a video game for five minutes reported that their mood improved. Those who either sat quietly without using a phone or computer or who participated in a guided relaxation activity did not report such improvement.

"We often try to power through the day to get more work finished, which might not be as effective as taking some time to detach for a few minutes," Rupp said in a release. "People should plan short breaks to make time for an engaging and enjoyable activity, such as video games, that can help them recharge."

In the study, the researchers gave 66 participants, 20 men and 46 women, an assessment to gauge their baseline mood. The participants then completed a computer-based task that induced cognitive fatigue and took another assessment. After that, they were given five minutes to rest. Participants were split into three groups: One group played the casual video game *Sushi Cat*, another participated in a guided relaxation activity, and the third sat quietly in the testing room without using a phone or computer. The researchers then assessed the participants a final time.

Participants who played the game showed a greater boost to their mood. Those who just sat quietly displayed a worse mood.

A 2014 study published in the *International Journal of Human-Computer Studies* found a positive correlation between time spent playing video games and recovering from work, as well as a reduction in work-related stress. First-person shooters and action games were most effective. These results were in line with a 2009 study published in the *Journal of CyberTherapy & Rehabilitation*.

It feels pretty good knowing that science supports my afternoon sessions of *Super Mario Run* in the office.

NINE RESEARCH-BACKED WAYS TO TURN AROUND A BAD DAY

John Rampton

No one is immune to a bad day. Upper management, fussy clients, a tumultuous home life, or possibly even a stressful, life-altering event can cause any one of us to have a bad day. Fortunately, we live in a modern era of scientific research centered on balanced living, health, and optimism.

We also have new technology that can aid in mental improvement, even for short-term fixes.

1. Binaural Beats

Binaural beats are brainwave technology that helps your brain get on a different wavelength and changes your state of mind. Research has proved binaural beats can train your brain and shift its course from a horrible mood to stress free and optimistic. Start off by listening to binaural beats passively, much like meditation. Download an app specifically designed for positive mood boosts, and tune into a frequency that boosts your mood back into the zone.

2. Try 7 Cups of Tea

No matter what your problem is, you can always find an app. The website 7 Cups of Tea (they also have an app) provides those wrestling with a difficult issue with an active, empathic listener. Talking about a problem creates new neural pathways in your brain, helping you heal and change habits, as well as come up with solutions and feel better.

Using an anonymous app is helpful because you don't want to overload your friends, family, or colleagues with your problems, making their day worse or creating tension with whoever may have caused you grief. If it's your boss that's the issue, for instance, venting to a co-worker actually can do more harm than good because they may bring it back to your manager.

3. Write a Thank-You Email

Sometimes the best way to turn your day around is to get outside yourself. Think about the last person who did something meaningful for you and send them a really specific thank-you note. Gratitude studies have shown writing down the things you're thankful for will increase optimism. By thinking about something someone did for you and sharing your gratitude, you will improve your own mood (and probably the mood of the other person as well).

I have also found that using this method in the sales process helps de-stress the people you're trying to get as clients.

4. Take a Quick Walk

When you're feeling angry or upset, one of the best solutions is to get moving. The blood will move away from your large muscle groups and limbs, where it flows when you're upset or angry due to our fight or flight instinct, and move back to your brain, so you can make better choices and problem solve. Walking will also release endorphins, calming you down.

5. Snack on Dark Chocolate

Dark chocolate provides mood-boosting benefits due to resveratrol (also found in red wine), which produces endorphins and serotonin. Be careful to keep it to one ounce per day, the amount for optimal health benefits. Buying a bag of dark chocolate snacks and keeping them in your desk may be a good solution—if you can limit yourself to one treat a day.

6. Meditate

Meditation has become the "in" exercise when it comes to reducing stress. It is becoming more and more common, with good reason, in corporate settings to have meditation rooms for employees to wind down and get focused. One study showed mindfulness meditation improves long-term focus and the ability to multitask, so adding meditation to your daily routine may allow you to deal with bad days more masterfully. All you need to start is two minutes spent clearing your brain and allowing yourself to refocus.

7. Take a Power Nap

Didn't get enough sleep last night? If you can make a quick escape to your car for a nap, you'll help beat the effects of stress and reset your system. A 20-minute nap will improve alertness and aid with motor functions. If you can get into the 30-60-minute zone, you can boost creativity and raise production once you get back to work. You can even use your binaural beats app to train your brain to enter the sleep cycle more quickly and efficiently.

8. Listen to a Stand-up Comedian

Laughter is the best medicine, especially when it comes to stress. Listening to a good stand-up routine from your favorite comedian will raise your oxygen intake, stimulate circulation, and lower your stress response. Jump on YouTube, Spotify, or whatever source you have, listen, and laugh.

9. Doctor on Demand

If your bad day becomes worse and you start to feel ill or panicked, or your bad days are turning into weeks or months, try Doctor on Demand. You can get an immediate appointment on your phone with a therapist whom you can video chat with and get expert advice on dealing with your stress. These doctors can write you a prescription, and if necessary they can direct you to a professional who can help you with coping skills during stressful times.

Having a bad day? Today, technology makes it easier than ever to turn your day around.

31

SCIENCE SHOWS HOW CREATIVITY CAN REDUCE STRESS

Deepak Chopra and Kabir Sehgal

Early in 2017, we grew anxious and distressed with how immigrants were being targeted with inflammatory rhetoric and discriminatory policies. But instead of taking to the streets to protest with anger, we got busy composing several songs, culminating in the release of our album *Home: Where Everyone Is Welcome*, which was inspired by immigrants. Rather than crying or complaining, we crooned. Indeed, the very act of creation—whether composing a song or starting a company—can help you redirect and reduce stress by using these negative feelings as catalysts to spark innovative ideas and products.

Creativity induces positive health effects, including on the heart. In one study, researchers provided almost 40 people with art supplies such as markers and paper and told them to create anything they wanted over a period of 45 minutes. The scientists discovered that no matter the artistic experience of the participants, about 75 percent experienced a decrease in their levels of cortisol, a hormone that the body secretes to respond to stress. "Everyone is creative and can be expressive in the visual arts when working in a supportive setting," explains one of the researchers.

This stress study is instructive because it implies that many of us could benefit from art therapy. Just like physical exercise, creative stimulation engages and focuses our minds on the task at hand—and distracts us from feelings of stress and anxiety.

When you create, you invoke your imagination, which is a productive and constructive use of your mind. By focusing intensely on a creative task, you can achieve the state of "flow," the term coined by psychologist Mihaly Csikszentmihalyi, and which is typically defined as the "optimal state of consciousness where we feel our best and perform our best."

In other words, when you "lose yourself" in the composition of a song or the drafting of an investor deck, you are essentially entering a healthy flow state. You don't notice time or events happening around you. According to acclaimed author Steven Kotler, during periods of flow, your brain secretes a healthy dose of pleasure-feeling chemicals such as dopamine, serotonin, and norepinephrine. By creating, we may enter flow, which can give us a rush of good feelings.

Perhaps we experience positive feelings because creation is ultimately an act of freedom. You manifest the world you want to see—one musical note or financial forecast at a time. In a study conducted by researchers at Johns Hopkins University, the brains of six accomplished jazz musicians were scanned while they improvised on a keyboard. The findings showed a decrease of activity in the region of the brain known as the dorsolateral prefrontal cortex, which is typically associated with thought, deliberation, and self-monitoring. This is the part of the brain you use when taking a tough exam or trying to interpret the words of a potential investor. The muted activity suggests that creativity—or, more precisely, improvisation—lowers your guard.

If you've seen a jazz musician improvise, you can't help but think they are in a state of flow, channeling inner emotions and rendering them into a beautiful melody. "What we think is happening is when you're telling your own musical story, you're shutting down impulses that might impede the flow of novel ideas," says one of the scientists. By creating, we feel freer and live without compunction.

Of course, not all of us are jazz musicians or songwriters. But we should still engage in a creative life—because we might live longer. In another study, researchers examined the data of 1,000 elderly men over a nearly 20-year period. They discovered that individuals who were more creative tended to live longer, presumably because creativity stimulates many regions of the brain, keeping it healthier.

"Individuals high in creativity maintain the integrity of their neural networks even into old age. . . . Keeping the brain healthy may be one of the most important aspects of aging successfully," says psychologist Nicholas Turiano, one of the researchers who is now a professor at West Virginia University. He also notes that creative people tend to handle stress better: "Creative people may see stressors more as challenges that they can work to overcome rather than as stressful obstacles they can't overcome."

When you're feeling down and out, get busy and creative. By putting yourself into a creative state, you'll be sweeping negative feelings to the corners of the room and making space for a new masterpiece—even if it's nothing to sing about!

TO THRIVE IN WORK AND LIFE, HERE'S WHAT SCIENCE SAYS YOU NEED

Nina Zipkin

You can quantify a company's success in terms of revenue, customer base, a high-profile acquisition, or an exit such as an IPO. But what about the more intangible qualities that make an individual prosperous, not just in terms of money or the workplace but in daily life?

A 2017 study conducted by the University of Portsmouth sought to define exactly what it means to thrive. Lead researcher Daniel Brown, a sports and exercise scientist, collected all the past research on the subject, including studies of successful artists, athletes, babies, and teenagers.

"It appears to come down to an individual experiencing a sense of development, of getting better at something, and succeeding at mastering something," Brown explained in a summary of the research. "In the simplest terms, what underpins it is feeling good about life and yourself and being good at something."

Brown identified a number of personal traits and outside circumstances that may lead someone to feel they are thriving. On the personality side, he noted that a thriving person is adaptable, flexible, motivated, optimistic, proactive, socially competent, and spiritual or religious. Those who thrive in their jobs tend to seek out information on developments in their field. They enjoy learning. They also believe in themselves, are resilient in the face of adversity, and have high self-esteem.

But Brown says people can't thrive on their personalities alone—they need external factors to bring out the best in them. Situations that offer a manageable balance of challenges and difficulties will "facilitate thriving." Other key factors include trusting interpersonal relationships with colleagues, employers, and family members that serve as a security blanket; a calm environment; a high degree of autonomy; and a reputation for being competent.

To thrive, people don't need to check all the boxes above, but some combination of these factors will stand them in good stead.

IF YOU'RE OPEN MINDED, RESEARCH SAYS YOU MIGHT DO THIS

Nina Zipkin

What does it mean to be "open-minded"? Most of us associate that term with being more tolerant of other perspectives, more intellectually curious, and more interested in different cultures and beliefs. Many entrepreneurs have an openness that allows them to problem solve and see potential where others might not think to look.

But according to a 2017 study from the University of Melbourne, people who are open minded not only *think* differently, they physically *see* the world around them differently from those who don't have that personality trait.

The researchers gave 123 participants a personality test that measured five elements—agreeableness, conscientiousness, extroversion, neuroticism, and openness to experience.

The idea behind the study was to better understand how being open minded relates to something called binocular rivalry—basically, when people are presented with two different images at the same time, one to each eye, they can only perceive one at a time.

In the experiment, the researchers showed contrasting images to the participants simultan-eously—a blob of red to one eye and a green blob to the other.

While most people's eyes went back and forth between the two, only able to register one color at a time, the researchers found that those who scored high on the "openness to experience" part of their personality tests were more likely to be able to perceive both colors at the same time—their eyes merged the colors together into one image.

What is happening in the brains of open-minded people? According to one of the Melbourne researchers, Luke Smillie, the culprit could be dopamine, which makes open people more sensitive to detecting and processing complex concepts. Another possibility is the relationship between openness and the brain's "default network," which Smillie describes as "a neural system that simulates various experiences such as mind wandering, mental time travel, and imagining others."

There is still a ton of research to be done on open-mindedness, but for now it would seem that allowing yourself to be open to new ideas at least enables you to see the world in new ways.

It would seem that if you are more open to possibilities, your physical ability to see can reflect that.

WHY TAKING A VACATION FROM MY BUSINESS EVERY YEAR IS GOOD FOR BUSINESS

Isaac Oates

"Work-life balance is easy," said no one ever. The truth is the mash-up of work and life has already happened. We are always on, always connected, always reachable. But we don't have to just live with this new reality. Instead, we can own it and make it as good as possible—and shape our own happiness.

And part of shaping your own happiness in work and life is knowing when you need to hit the pause button.

I try to take a summer vacation every year, giving myself time off to travel and reflect. This year in Paris and Berlin, I was able to fully unplug and spend time hanging out with my son, as well as reading, reflecting, and rejuvenating—to me, the critical three R's of a meaningful vacation. Critical, because those three R's are what allow me to come back to my desk refreshed and ready (two more R's) to lead my team.

The benefits of taking time off—and the risks of *not* doing so—are well-documented. Research shows that work exhaustion without sufficient recovery time increases the odds of health and safety issues. Overwork is a detriment to both ourselves and our companies. It can lead to health problems like impaired sleep, depression, heavy drinking, diabetes, impaired memory, and heart disease. For companies, that all equates to disengaged or absent employees, high turnover, and rising health-care costs.

And working more doesn't actually accomplish more—working more than 50 hours per week cuts deeply into productivity, and productivity drops off completely after 55 hours.

Ultimately, we've all felt it: Trying to push forward and ignore exhaustion cuts down on our ability to persevere, to bounce back from difficult days, and to feel invested in the work we do.

It's not surprising, then, that employees overwhelmingly rank work-life balance and flexible companies as a major draw. A 2017 Justworks survey found that 42 percent of employees would take a lower-paying job if it offered a greater degree of workplace flexibility. And according to research conducted with Fortune 500 companies, employees with higher work flexibility "voiced higher levels of job satisfaction and reduced levels of burnout and psychological stress" than those with less flexibility.

While true work-life balance can be hard to achieve, business owners can encourage their teams to unplug in order to boost employee happiness, engagement, and productivity. We offer unlimited PTO at Justworks to encourage people to take time off and restore the balance in their lives. We've built a culture where staff can feel like their teams are more than capable of covering for them when they take those breaks.

Even if unlimited vacation policies may not be feasible for your company, encouraging staff to take PTO and recharge is beneficial for both your business and your employees. And trying to make sure people fully unplug by discouraging "working vacations" and limiting work outside of work hours can go a long way toward minimizing employee exhaustion.

You could also consider offering perks like flexible hours or the option to work from home to give employees a little extra freedom and headspace without any sacrifice to the company. That kind of flexibility also helps communicate your appreciation for their hard work when they *are* working. And by giving your team more say in the terms of their commitment to your company, you can help them feel more empowered and actually strengthen that commitment.

I'm lucky enough to love what I do. I love what we're building here at Justworks. I love our mission to free entrepreneurs who are serious about taking care of their teams to focus on building their businesses and making them a great place to work. But even when you're in love, you need space for yourself. I know that unplugging and taking real time off always helps me come back with renewed energy and a fresh perspective. I encourage my team to do the same, and to make sure their time off is just as meaningful as their time in the office.

But it's not just altruism—I know that our company benefits, too, when our employees take the time to recharge.

SCIENCE KNOWS YOU NEED TO GET A LIFE OUTSIDE OF WORK

John Rampton

If you're like most employed Americans, the majority of your day—close to nine hours—is spent working. If you're like most entrepreneurs (including myself), add three to four hours to that number.

That doesn't leave a whole lot of time for socializing, spending time with your family, working on a hobby or passion project, or just kicking back and relaxing. Even worse? Americans are putting off retirement by continuing to work into their 70s and 80s.

Is this because we're workaholics? Not exactly.

Unlike most other countries around the world, we don't put an emphasis on having a life aside from our jobs. While factors like a low minimum wage and having too little set aside for retirement play a part, we don't have laws guaranteeing vacation time or paternity/maternity leave. Employers discourage longer lunch breaks and *really* don't want employees to unplug.

That's a major problem. Overworked employees are less productive, more prone to burn out, and less likely to be loyal to the organization. Additionally, research has found that the most satisfied employees are those who have a life outside the office.

Why You Need to Get a Life (Outside of Work)

Let's get real here. Whether you're an entrepreneur, freelancer, or nine-to-fiver, jobs will come and go due to business failure, losing clients, or outgrowing your current position. If your identity and happiness depend on your job, what happens if that abruptly disappears? What happens if you end up with a toxic new boss?

"When your job defines you, your world becomes very narrow. Thoughts about your job and the challenges you face are always on your mind no matter what you're doing or whom you're with," writes Ray Williams, author of *Eye of the Storm: How Mindful Leaders Can Transform Chaotic Workplaces, Leadership Edge,* and *Breaking Bad Habits.*

"You subtly begin to value people, activities, and relationships based solely on how they can help your career. And you consistently withdraw your time, talent, and energy from other areas of your life so that you can give more of yourself to your work, leaving you emotionally empty outside the office. When your job defines you, everything that happens at work seems personal," he adds.

Working long hours can hurt your relationships. One study in the U.K. found that poor work-life balance is the third-biggest strain on relationships. That's understandable. If you're working all the time, that makes your spouse responsible for things like household chores and taking care of your children. There isn't enough quality time for the two of you.

There are also serious health implications to overwork, including poor sleep, risk of depression, and increased risk of heart disease.

This might surprise the workaholics, but a life outside of work helps you become more successful and productive in your professional life. Taking a breather from work reduces stress, clears your head, and reenergizes you. Spending time with people, traveling, and learning something new can help you bring new perspectives to your work, boost your creativity, and develop new skills.

Maybe you're thinking, "I get it. It's important to have a life outside the office, but that's just not possible for me." It is if you follow these tips.

Set Boundaries Based on Your Priorities

Some days you have to work long hours, but you need to set clear boundaries so it doesn't happen every day. Don't make new commitments when you already have a full plate. Don't schedule a meeting the afternoon you know you have to be out the door on time to attend to a personal obligation. Don't volunteer to take on a new assignment if you have to be at the kids' ball game.

Tell Everyone When You're Not Available

You can't establish your boundaries if no one knows about them. If you're going on vacation, tell your clients now. If you have to leave by 5:30 P.M., inform your colleagues and manager in the morning so they won't throw any last-minute assignments your way.

Stop Trying to Be Perfect

Nothing is ever perfect. Do your best and move on. This is easier said than done, but you have to do it. Instead of aiming for perfection, I do it the best I can and then reevaluate a few weeks later when I have data to tell me how well I did!

Unplug

Turn off your phone when you're eating dinner, going out with friends, and going to bed. If you don't, work will keep distracting you from enjoying the moment. I like to keep 6 P.M. to 8 P.M. every night as a distraction-free time so I can spend it with my family. Learn to unplug.

Exercise and Meditate

Both of these activities keep us mentally and physically healthy, reduce stress, and help us sleep. You're busy, but you can still find five or ten minutes to meditate or exercise daily. I go on daily walks to clear my mind and come up with new ideas.

Limit Distractions

Reduce the number of distractions you have during working hours. Turn off email and social media notifications. Reply to phone calls and emails in batches, not as they come in. Don't chitchat with colleagues. The sooner you get work finished, the sooner you're done for the day.

Automate and Delegate

Automate recurring processes like social media updates and recurring invoices. If you have a business, consider outsourcing some tasks to freelancers, like accounting or writing blog posts to reduce your daily workload.

A life outside of work is imperative to becoming a happier, more productive, and successful individual. Start small and begin to ascend on a slow, steady course, instead of going all-in at once.

Here's to having an amazing life outside of work!

FIVE SCIENCE-BACKED WAYS TO BE HAPPIER AT WORK

Kim Lachance Shandrow

Google "How to be happier" and before you're even finished typing, "How to be happier at work" is among the top three suggestions to pop up. Happiness at work is evidently on a lot of people's minds, considering that search term's popularity on Google, a company that has employed a chief happiness officer. (Check out his business card. He's literally a "Jolly Good Fellow.")

Why wouldn't feeling happier at work be at the top of our collective consciousness? After all, most of us spend a third of our days working. Our time on the clock might as well be pleasant and fulfilling.

If it's not, if you're a sad, sullen downer of a worker—and your boss could very well be on to this—studies suggest that you're significantly more likely to slack off. On top of the emotional toll on your own well-being, your blues could also be a costly drain on your company's bottom line and seriously bum out those who work around you.

On the upside, a growing body of data suggests that being happier at work can make you more engaged, less likely to quit, and better at collaborating, among many other benefits. Generally speaking, the happier you are, the better your brain works and the better you feel and perform at work, says Emiliana Simon-Thomas, a veteran neuroscientist and the science director of the Greater Good Science Center at UC Berkeley.

"When workers are happier, they're healthier and accomplish more," she says. "They tend to enjoy their relationships at work and elsewhere. They work better on teams. They're more well-liked by their co-workers and they're more immune to burnout. So if I'm an employer, helping them feel happier on my watch isn't even a hard sell. Putting happiness where the vision and mission are, it's a given."

While earning her doctorate in brain cognition and behavior at UC Berkeley, she focused on how negative states such as fear and aversion influence thinking and decision making. Now she mainly studies happiness and the behaviors that generate the feel-good emotion.

Simon-Thomas is also the co-creator and co-teacher of a free eight-week edX online course titled "The Science of Happiness." I should mention, in the interest of full disclosure, that I have taken the class.

I spoke with her about her top five tips for being happier at work, for both employers and employees. Here they are:

1. Bring Your Personal Baggage to Work

"The professional culture norm has long been to leave your personal baggage at home. You come in. You do work. We don't always know if our co-workers are parents. We don't know if they are caring for others who demand a lot of their time and energy outside work. We often don't know much about our co-workers and what they're personally going through.

"What researchers are realizing is that the separation of professional and personal is a poor model. It minimizes workers in a way that makes it more difficult for them to be happy, to feel valuable, connected, trusted, and cared for at work. It's time to promote empathy in the workplace, to ask questions and feature opportunities for employees to share their real-life moments. A good starting place is to have off-site play days for your staff, when they can talk about who they really are, what they're really about, and where they really come from. Knowing that information about your co-workers, like if they're in the midst of a challenging personal situation, which we all go through, can be helpful to understanding where the person is coming from. It promotes compassion and happiness, and it puts money in your company's bank in terms of trust and social connections."

Bottom line: Getting personal at the office increases co-worker trust and compassion.

2. Stop Competing With Co-Workers

"Work is often framed as being something you earn. Maybe others think you were the lucky one who got a new position, or a raise, or maybe you're the most qualified one. It's very competitive, and people get jealous and harbor resentment. Workplace competition is counter to cooperation, as it creates a sense of holding on to what's yours and making sure nobody else intrudes upon your territory.

"In actuality, and empirically speaking, that mentality is not as productive. It doesn't lend itself to happiness, nor to the type of achievement that stems from the cooperation of your teammates.

"Instead, break down departmental silos. Don't act like rivals. Help each other. Create a culture of happiness, cooperation, and an open idea- and resource-sharing environment. Make it the norm. People naturally work together much better when they're not pitted against each other."

Bottom line: Teamwork makes the dream work.

3. Take a Breather

"Taking a deep breath as often as you can at work, or having some kind of extra awareness of what's going on in your own psychological milieu, is so important. Engaging in mindful habits, like breathing deeply before meetings or on break or whenever you can fit it in, can reduce the toxic rumination and racing thoughts that often lead to stress and anxiety—the things that ultimately take our minds off work and render us less productive.

"Focus on your breath when you're in a moment of reactivity, when you're tempted to perhaps yell at someone about something they did that irritates you. Notice the urge, get curious about it, feel the joy of letting go, and repeat.

"Instead of being like, 'Oh, no, I'm not going to scream at that person!' and then avoiding that feeling and replacing it with something else, perhaps panic, work on your awareness and breathe through it. You don't have to [do it] in a way that is so heavy handed that you meditate right then and there. Just take that inhale and breathe it out slowly and notice where your urges are. If you have the urge to lash out, consider the possibilities. You probably won't feel better after, and lashing out won't work at work. Breathing will."

Bottom line: Stop, think, and breathe in the heat of the moment.

4. Express Gratitude for People

"Gratitude has been proven to present a huge opportunity for increasing happiness. There are lots of opportunities at work to be grateful for the people you work with. It's up to you to show it, to vocally, explicitly express gratitude to the co-workers and teammates who make your livelihood, progress, and daily efforts possible.

"Expressing thanks and showing you're grateful for them brings about a deep, mutual sense of belonging and cohesion. It also creates empathy and trust in the workplace, which is essential to accomplishing collective work goals together. The giver and the receiver will feel a sense of purpose, a sense of camaraderie, and like they matter in the bigger scheme of the enterprise.

"This one especially applies to bosses, who often feel, 'I don't have to thank my employees because I'm paying them.' Thank each other, no matter where you are on the organizational chart. It goes a long way, starting at the top, where leaders can model gratitude, and not with employee-of-the-month programs that can cause animosity. It could be as simple as taking a few seconds to pop your head into someone's office and saying thank you to them for expending their life energy to make your business successful."

Bottom line: Saying "Thank you" is more than just good manners.

5. Play Nice

"Just be nice, as simple as it sounds. It's one of the most measurably effective things you can do to easily and immediately increase happiness at work. Researchers saw this in a recent nursing industry organizational trust study and intervention. The nurses who took part were burning out and unhappy.

"To the surprise of the researchers, the nurses weren't burning out because of the long hours and pay and compensation issues. What was really heard loud and clear: There was a culture of incivility that everyone was grappling with—a habit and culture of being unkind, competitive, snarky, and hostile to each other. In working through those systemic causes of unhappiness, and learning to be simply nice to each other, the nurses were eventually able to come to a place of well-being."

Bottom line: Be kind, don't be cutthroat, and lay off the snark.

FOUR THINGS SCIENCE SAYS YOU CAN DO TO BE HAPPY

John Boitnott

People spend years chasing happiness, only to learn the hard way that it wasn't where they thought it was. They assume career success, riches, retirement, or the "perfect relationship" will bring the happiness they've always wanted. In the process, they miss the enjoyable moments all around them.

But what will make you happy? To find out, we turned to one of the best resources available today. Stanford University's Center for Compassion and Altruism Research and Education has devoted considerable effort to studying "the positive qualities of the human mind." In the process, the team at Stanford regularly releases studies that quantify happiness. Here are four things they have learned over the past few years.

1. Be Compassionate

Stanford has a long-standing research interest in the connection between practicing compassion and achieving happiness. The center offers an eight-week course called Compassion Cultivation Training (CCT) that teaches attendees how to develop a more compassionate attitude. In a study to determine the program's usefulness, they found it led to an increase in both mindfulness and happiness. The training, the study authors said, emphasizes the benefits of connecting with fellow human beings to a person's overall well-being.

You don't have to spend every weekend doing charity work to achieve happiness, however. Simply find ways in your everyday life to be more compassionate. Listen to others when they're speaking and truly work to see things from other people's perspectives.

2. Spend Time in Nature

When was the last time you took a walk through the park or spent the afternoon by the pool? While it's important to minimize sun exposure, Mother Nature brings many benefits, both physical and emotional. One of those benefits is an improved affect, according to a study led by Stanford University's Gregory N. Bratman.

The study separated participants into two groups: one that spent their outdoor time in urban settings and a second that took nature walks. Those who took the nature walk showed a marked improvement in overall well-being, including a decrease in anxiety and worry. If you don't have easy access to a hiking area, consider taking your lunch to a nearby park or waterfront.

3. Disconnect from Social Media

People are constantly connected to other people through social media, even when they're trying to enjoy "alone time." Stanford University psychology researchers set out to determine just how contagious negativity is. Unfortunately, people aren't as good at guessing the moods of others as we might think they are. The researchers discovered that people overestimate how happy other people are, leading them to assume that other people's lives are better than they actually are.

Social media is especially dangerous to happiness. Time spent on social media has been connected to a prevalence of depression and anxiety. Make a concerted effort to stay off social media, especially if you find yourself unfavorably comparing yourself to others. As a test, try to stay away for a few days and see if your mood begins to improve.

4. Search for Meaning

Philosophers have long pondered the meaning of life, and they aren't the only ones. One Stanford study attempted to find the link between meaningfulness and happiness and found that while they're different, they also overlap. Someone can find meaningfulness while still being unhappy. For instance, someone may find great meaning in their work as an activist or social worker but still feel unhappy.

At the same time, someone who is self-involved may find that he or she feels happy while living a life without much meaning. It's important to look for ways to live a meaningful life while also finding what makes you happy. Based on the results of the study, some things that make people happier include focusing on the present rather than the past or future and spending time with those who make you feel happy.

Happiness is not easily defined, but science tells us what has been shown to boost our own well-being. Each person's definition of happiness will differ, so it's most important to find the key to happiness for you and eliminate the obstacles that are keeping you from living the happiest life you can.

ENTREPRENEUR VOICES SPOTLIGHT: INTERVIEW WITH JASON WOMACK

CEO of The Womack Company

When Jason Womack was a high school teacher back in the 1990s, he had so much work and so little free time that he tried to train himself to sleep just four hours a night. "This is when I knew something had to change," he says. "It just wasn't sustainable." That search for change resulted in a career devoted to helping other busy professionals better manage their time and be more productive.

As CEO of The Womack Company, an international training firm, and co-author (with his wife) of *Get Momentum: How to Start When You're Stuck*, Womack has coached people across industries in how to get things done without losing sleep over it.

Entrepreneur: How important is it to balance your daily schedule between "work" and "life"? What percentage of time should you give each endeavor?

Womack: I'm one of those guys who goes "all-in." If I'm working, you're going to see an intensity and drive that walk along a line you'd call perfectionistic and overachieving. If you see me racing an Olympic-distance triathlon, you'll see that everything I've got is right here, right now; I'll give you 95 to 97 percent of my heart rate for those 21/2 hours. And if you catch me sleeping, well, of all the guys that I've interviewed, I constantly rate at the top of deep sleep/light sleep/awake metrics through each night.

Now, my daily schedule needs to reflect the movement [not balance] between living . . . and making a living. It's really challenging for me to give you a percentage, so here's what I'd say:

Divide your day into natural sections, blocks of time that mean something to you. Think about times of the day you need to think, plan, visualize, and discuss the future. At other times of the day you need to "work." Make the calls, write the emails, talk to people one-on-one or in small groups, or read and review the documentation you're studying. Then there will be other times of the day you need to relax, recharge, and refresh. Make sure you take care of your *body* and *mind* needs—this way you can come back stronger and more focused than ever before.

Entrepreneur: You're a bike racer and triathlete. How much time do you devote to those activities? And why do you think it makes a difference in your overall success?

Womack: I schedule my workouts 15 to 30 days in advance. Every Sunday, I review and renegotiate those workouts based on what city I am in, where I'm traveling, and scheduled athletic events. Personally, I need something to train for. The people who can just exercise because they're supposed to amaze me! I'll always have two to three events (a half marathon, a triathlon, a Rim-to-Rim-to-Rim hike at the Grand Canyon . . .) on the calendar!

A workout is an hour—unless it isn't! That's why I schedule them so far in advance. I know on a travel day, to get that 60-minute session in will be a challenge. And on the weekend, the two-hour run and one-hour bike ride won't happen if I just hope I have time. Now how does all this help me overall? Well, the first part is what I shared earlier: I need a goal, something to go toward that has an objective finish line. When I step on that treadmill for a two-hour indoor training session, I'm not bothered by the fact that I'll be in one place for 120 minutes; I'm training to make it to the finish line of an upcoming event. Too many times entrepreneurs start with goals that aren't objective enough, and they aren't 100 percent willing to do the long, boring, unglamorous, behind-the-scenes work.

In my business life, as a writer, author, and coach, I've found that my hardest projects are the ones where I don't have clear goals. I'll work overtime, stay up late, and get up early to clarify not just the goal but iterative milestones that I can take on that will get me closer to what I want.

Entrepreneur: You have a lot of things going on in your day. How do you prioritize?

Womack: In our book *Get Momentum: How to Start When You're Stuck*, Jodi and I give you a great prioritization tactic called the #KnownFor exercise. If you happen to read that book and make it to chapter three, you'll read the question we give you there: "What do you want to be known for?" This question is not meant to freak you out or make you rethink your life. Instead, we ask you to bring it down to more immediate and more practical levels.

Here's how:

- *Step one*. Identify 8 to 15 roles you have at work and in life. My own examples (of course!) would include: Author, Husband, Executive Coach, Triathlete, Volunteer, Keynote Speaker, and Homeowner.

- *Step two*. For each role, pick a particular project/event/milestone that is 6 to 12 months out. I like that time frame because it gets me OUT of the day-to-day overwhelm and into thinking about what those MOST important things are.

- *Step three*. Write a three-to-five-sentence #Known For statement for each.

It could look like this:

As an author, by September 10, I want to be known for submitting a book proposal to my publisher. I want the proposed idea to be exciting enough for me to want to write about AND tested by and in the market I'm writing to. I want to be known as an author who constantly brings new and useful things to readers worldwide.

My job now is to review those #KnownFor statements "as often as I need to so that I'm working on my priorities." How often is that? Honestly, I've found the best cadence for me is every couple of days.

Entrepreneur: You've said the hardest part of your job is to decide what NOT to do every day. How do you do it?

Womack: First off, I gotta know what shouldn't be on the list anymore. That's where the #KnownFor process kicks in. To-dos and even projects have a sneaky way of making it to the list of things we think we should do. Check your calendar, your email inbox, and today's list. About once a week (Thursdays for me), I stop working for about 30 minutes, maybe an hour. And for that time, I go through every inventory of "work" I've collected that week. My goal?

To get rid of 50 percent of what is there! I will tell you the challenge, ready? While I'm cleaning up, I always see something that I added to my list and think, "Oh, it'll just take a couple of minutes, I'll do it right now." Then I watch a couple of short videos, read a few saved articles, draft a short 250-word article for one of the magazines/websites I write for. I make a phone call or two, even type out an email. And then . . .

And THEN, I'm right where I was before.

So no! My job during this cleanup process is to look at a list of ten things and get rid of five of them. I may delegate two, delete two, and move one five to eight weeks out on the calendar. I do anything I can to clean up my system so that I know what I am doing, have to do, and can get by without doing.

Entrepreneur: What advice would you give to those so-called "workaholics" who think success lies in the number of hours you put toward your work?

Womack: I looked up that word in the dictionary and found "a person who compulsively works hard and long hours." I'm not here to judge if you're working hard (and not smart) or long hours. I've met people who have a position, situation, or circumstance that demands they work 10 to 12 to 15 hours a day. My question is always one of sustainability. That is, can you work 15-hour days—for a career?

There are going to be projects you're on and events you're a part of that dictate you work hard and long. Alternatively, there is other work you have to do that could be easier! Here's my advice: Look at your #KnownFor statements that I wrote about earlier. Go back through them, and add how you want to be known as being, not just doing. If you know you get tempted to work long, hard hours, put something in there about working efficiently, asking for help early on in your projects, and getting things done in the time that you promised.

One of the main reasons people work long, hard hours is they give themselves too much time to get things done. Instead of telling yourself you'll have that "thing" (whatever it is) done by Friday next week, set a timer for 30, 60, or 90 minutes, and go all out on it right now.

Wanna prove me wrong? Go ahead! I shared earlier that a well-placed question just may change everything. So

I'll ask you: "What's the question you need to ask yourself to take what you do and how you do it to the next level?"

MINDSETS THAT CREATE BALANCE— REFLECTIONS

The way we've been working isn't working. Most of us are putting in longer hours with shorter breaks and have very little to show for it—except stress, frustration, and fatigue. This stems from both the deeply ingrained notion that success equals working day and night, and the fact that technology makes it easier than ever to work day and night. Damn you, technology.

Here's the bad news: Being a so-called workaholic is not a badge of honor. It's a badge of horror. Research shows that work exhaustion can lead to impaired sleep, depression, diabetes, and heart disease—not to mention being less effective and less productive. The good news is that research is also showing us the power of balancing our work with our so-called "life." New science is proving that stepping away from your desk and doing something different, or even doing nothing at all, is beneficial not only for your health but your business.

Breaks are a necessity, not a luxury. Playing video games at five-minute intervals may seem like a guilty pleasure, but it's actually been shown to help you recharge your energy and improve your mood. Reporting for Call of Duty, sir! In fact, taking brief breaks to snack on some dark chocolate, unplug and meditate, do something creative like paint, or listen to binaural beats on your AirPods has been scientifically proved to reduce stress and increase productivity. And it's not just short breaks that are beneficial; longer vacations are also highly recommended. Research shows that work exhaustion without adequate time for recovery can lead to emotional exhaustion as well. According to one study, spending time in nature reduces stress and actually improves memory.

Turn off your smartphone, close your laptop, and take an inventory of yourself. Are you feeling burned out? Is your stress level off the charts? If the answers are yes and yes, that's your body and mind telling you it's time to shift your attention away from work and toward your own well-being. Remember that creepy phrase Jack Nicholson types again and again in the movie *The Shining*? "All work and no play makes Jack a dull boy." Science shows work without play not only makes you a dull boy (or girl), it makes you an unhealthy and unhappy one, too.

RESOURCES

(in order of appearance)

Thank you to our talented Entrepreneur contributors whose content is featured in this book. For more information about these contributors, including author bios, visit us at www.entrepreneur.com.

1. Entrepreneur Staff, "Nine Science-Backed Insights on Finding Success in Your Business and Personal Life," *Entrepreneur*, June 5, 2017, http://entrepreneur.com/article/294582.

2. Kate Rockwood, "Science-Backed Brain Hacks to Crush Your Goals," *Entrepreneur*, January 11, 2017, http://entrepreneur.com/article/286912.

3. Rose Leadem, "Why You Should Stop Saying Sorry, According to Science," *Entrepreneur*, September 8, 2017, http://entrepreneur.com/article/300055.

4. Deep Patel, "Nine Habits of Highly Innovative People," *Entrepreneur*, June 6, 2018, www.entrepreneur.com/article/313733.

5. Chirag Kulkarni, "The Seven Things Science Says You Must Do Daily to Build a Billion Dollar Business," *Entrepreneur*, September 8, 2016, www.entrepreneur.com/article/281310.

6. John Rampton, "Neuroscience Tells Us How to Hack Our Brains for Success," *Entrepreneur*, June 16, 2017, http://entrepreneur.com/article/295885.

7. Lydia Belanger, "Seven Science-Backed Strategies for Building Powerful Habits," *Entrepreneur*, February 23, 2017, http://entrepreneur.com/article/289564.

8. Murray Newlands, "Four Science-Backed Ways to Increase Productivity," *Entrepreneur*, October 21, 2016, http://entrepreneur.com/article/282936.

9. Jennifer L. Gibbs and Terri R. Kurtzberg, "Science Says Our Constant Connectivity Is Hurting Productivity. Here's How to Fix It." *Entrepreneur*, June 20, 2017, http://entrepreneur.com/article/295863.

10. Thai Nguyen, "Science Knows the Two-Step Process for Breaking the Bad Habits Holding You Back," *Entrepreneur*, June 13, 2017, http://entrepreneur.com/article/295465.

11. Ahmed Safwan, "Five Bad Habits You Must Change to Be More Productive," *Entrepreneur*, April 3, 2017, http://entrepreneur.com/article/290498.

12. John Stevens, "Five Research-Backed Strategies to Increase Your Sales Revenues," *Entrepreneur*, June 21, 2016, http://entrepreneur.com/article/276815.

13. John Stevens, "Five Research-Backed Tips to Increase Online Sales," *Entrepreneur*, August 3, 2016, http://entrepreneur.com/article/279695.

14. John Boitnott, "Science Warns Don't Do These Six Things If You Want to Get Hired," *Entrepreneur*, July 4, 2017, http://entrepreneur.com/article/296737.

15. Taddy Hall and Linda Deeken, "Five Steps to Getting Your Brand 'Hired' in the Real World,"

Entrepreneur, April 26, 2017, http://entrepreneur.com/article/293230.

16. Carolyn Sun, "The Science of the First Impression: Five Elements of a Great First Impression," *Entrepreneur*, March 13, 2018, www.entrepreneur.com/slideshow/309948.

17. Jeffery Lindenmuth, Ross McCammon, and Kate Rockwood, "Closing a Deal at a Bar? This Research Can Help." *Entrepreneur*, June 27, 2016, http://entrepreneur.com/article/277815.

18. Stephen J. Bronner, "Eight Science-Backed Techniques That Will Make You More Likeable," *Entrepreneur*, August 25, 2016, http://entrepreneur.com/article/281401.

19. Nina Zipkin, "Science Just Gave Us Another Reason Not to Use Emoji at Work," *Entrepreneur*, August 14, 2017, http://entrepreneur.com/article/298723.

20. Lesya Liu, "Researchers Find That Social Media Can Make You Happier or Miserable," *Entrepreneur*, April 17, 2017, http://entrepreneur.com/article/292526.

21. Michael Cooper, "Motivate Customers to Buy Based on Their Brand Type," *Entrepreneur*,

November 3, 2014, www.entrepreneur.com/article/237662.

22. Chris Poelma, "Analyzing the Science Behind Customer Loyalty," *Entrepreneur*, May 13, 2016, http://entrepreneur.com/article/272038.

23. Dan Blacharski, "The Art of Persuading Customers to Tell Your Story Is Becoming a Science," *Entrepreneur*, October 12, 2016, http://entrepreneur.com/article/282633.

24. Eric Samson, "The Science Behind High-Converting Websites," *Entrepreneur*, June 8, 2016, http://entrepreneur.com/article/276268.

25. Brian Sutter, "Five Ways to Maximize Word-of-Mouth Marketing," *Entrepreneur*, November 6, 2015, http://entrepreneur.com/article/251576.

26. Jonathan Long, "Five Simple Tips You Can Use to Capture the Attention of Millennials," *Entrepreneur*, October 2, 2017, http://entrepreneur.com/article/301148.

27. Tobi Abdulgafar, "Seven Science-Backed Strategies for Dealing With Angry Customers," *Entrepreneur*, March 30, 2017, http://entrepreneur.com/article/290788.

28. Luc Burgelman, "The Science Behind Customer Churn," *Entrepreneur*, April 20, 2016, http://entrepreneur.com/article/270774.

29. Stephen J. Bronner, "Stressed Out? Science Says to Play a Video Game for Five Minutes." *Entrepreneur*, July 27, 2017, http://entrepreneur.com/article/297881.

30. John Rampton, "Nine Ways Backed by Research to Turn Around a Bad Day," *Entrepreneur*, June 30, 2015, http://entrepreneur.com/article/247835.

31. Deepak Chopra and Kabir Sehgal, "Science Shows How Creativity Can Reduce Stress," *Entrepreneur*, September 15, 2017, http://entrepreneur.com/article/300347.

32. Nina Zipkin, "To Thrive in Work and Life, Here's What Science Says You Need," *Entrepreneur*, September 11, 2017, http://entrepreneur.com/article/300116.

33. Nina Zipkin, "If You're Open Minded, Research Says You Might Do This," *Entrepreneur*, June 5, 2017, http://entrepreneur.com/article/295346.

34. Isaac Oates, "I Take a Vacation From My Business Every Year. Research Shows Why It's Good for Me—and My Company." *Entrepreneur*,

August 22, 2017, http://entrepreneur.com/article/298888.

35. John Rampton, "Science Knows You Need to Get a Life Outside of Work. This Is How You Do It." *Entrepreneur*, April 28, 2017, http://entrepreneur.com/article/293500.

36. Kim Lachance Shandrow, "Five Science-Backed Ways to Be Happier at Work," *Entrepreneur*, May 26, 2016, http://entrepreneur.com/article/276522.

37. John Boitnott, "Four Things Science Says You Can Do to Be Happy," *Entrepreneur*, September 6, 2017, http://entrepreneur.com/article/299692.

Reader's Notes

_____

_____

_____

_____

_____

_____

_____

_____

_____

_____

_____

_____

_____

_____

_____

_____

_____

Reader's Notes

_____

_____

_____

_____

_____

_____

_____

_____

_____

_____

_____

_____

_____

_____

_____

_____

_____